KU-655-742

WHIRLWIND

THE INCREDIBLE STORY OF

JIMMY WHITE

LIBRARIES NI
WITHDRAWN FROM STOCK

Aubrey Malone

KNOW THE SCORE BOOKS SPORTS PUBLICATIONS

CULT HEROES	Author	ISBN
CARLISLE UNITED	Paul Harrison	978-1-905449-09-7
CELTIC	David Potter	978-1-905449-08-8
CHELSEA	Leo Moynihan	1-905449-00-3
MANCHESTER CITY	David Clayton	978-1-905449-05-7
NEWCASTLE	Dylan Younger	1-905449-03-8
NOTTINGHAM FOREST	David McVay	978-1-905449-06-4
RANGERS	Paul Smith	978-1-905449-07-1
SOUTHAMPTON	Jeremy Wilson	1-905449-01-1
WEST BROM	Simon Wright	1-905449-02-X

MATCH OF MY LIFE	Editor	ISBN
BRIGHTON	Paul Camillin	978-1-84818-000-0
DERBY COUNTY	Nick Johnson	978-1-905449-68-2
ENGLAND WORLD CUP	Massarella & Moynihan	1-905449-52-6
EUROPEAN CUP FINALS	Ben Lyttleton	1-905449-57-7
FA CUP FINALS 1953-1969	David Saffer	978-1-905449-53-8
FULHAM	Michael Heatley	1-905449-51-8
IPSWICH TOWN	Mel Henderson	978-1-84818-001-7
LEEDS	David Saffer	1-905449-54-2
LIVERPOOL	Leo Moynihan	1-905449-50-X
MANCHESTER UNITED	Ivan Ponting	978-1-905449-59-0
SHEFFIELD UNITED	Nick Johnson	1-905449-62-3
STOKE CITY	Simon Lowe	978-1-905449-55-2
SUNDERLAND	Rob Mason	1-905449-60-7
WOLVES	Simon Lowe	1-905449-56-9

PLAYER BY PLAYER	Author	ISBN
LIVERPOOL	Ivan Ponting	978-1-84818-306-3
MANCHESTER UNITED	Ivan Ponting	978-1-84818-500-1
TOTTENHAM HOTSPUR	Ivan Ponting	978-1-84818-501-8

GREATEST GAMES	Author	ISBN
SCOTLAND	David Potter	978-1-84818-200-4
STOKE CITY	Simon Lowe & David Lee	978-1-84818-201-1
WEST BROM	Simon Wright	978-1-84818-206-6

GENERAL FOOTBALL	Author	ISBN
A GREAT FACE FOR RADIO	John Anderson	978-1-84818-403-9
A SMASHING LITTLE FOOTBALL FIRM	Nicky Allt	978-1-84818-402-2

WHIRLWIND

THE INCREDIBLE STORY OF
JIMMY WHITE

Aubrey Malone

www.knowthescorebooks.com

First published in the United Kingdom

by Know The Score Books Ltd, 2009

Copyright Aubrey Malone

This book is copyright under the Berne convention.

No part of this book may be reproduced, sold or utilised in any form or transmitted in any form or by any means, electronic or mechanical, including photocopying, recording or by any information storage and retrieval system, without prior permission in writing from the Publisher.

© Aubrey Malone, 2009

The right of Aubrey Malone to be identified as the author of this work has been asserted by him in accordance with sections 77 and 78 of the Copyright, Designs and Patents Act, 1988.

Know The Score Books Limited
118 Alcester Road
Studley
Warwickshire
B80 7NT
01527 454482
info@knowthescorebooks.com
www.knowthescorebooks.com

A CIP catalogue record is available for this book from the British Library
ISBN: 978-1-84818-742-9

By

LIBRARIES NI	
C700203201	
RONDO	20/01/2010
794.735092	£ 14.99
PST	

CONTENTS

To Jimmy, the best world champion snooker never had.
If you left something to error, it only made
you even more compulsive.

PREFACE

MY WIFE MARY all too often had to suffer me going into a downer every time Jimmy White lost a snooker match.

She knew he was a great player and a lovely lad, but at the end of the day what did it matter if he won or lost? It was a recreational sport. It was meant to be enjoyed, for God's sake. *Why did I put myself through the pain barrier like that?* I was asked over and over again. This isn't a war, isn't a cure for cancer, doesn't split the atom, isn't the Third Secret of Fatima.

"This is going beyond the beyonds," she said to me one night when I was almost chewing the carpet with rage after Jimmy missed a pot that would have won him a match. "You've got no life of your own any more. It's all wrapped up in that idiot. I wish he was never born."

This was heresy.

"How can you say that?" I asked, distraught. "You know how good Jimmy makes me feel when he wins."

"Yes," she stormed back, "like once a year."

"That's beneath the belt!" I shouted.

"You say it yourself all the time," she countered, painfully accurately. "Are you saying it's okay for you to give out about him but not me? That's sexist."

Mary told me that he was almost becoming like a religion to me, that I needed to break out of the bubble that was Jimmy.

Maybe she was right.

Maybe I wasn't really as obsessed with him as I thought I was, or wanted to be. Maybe I just needed something or someone to be fixated on.

Maybe, I thought, I should set up a society called Snookeraholics Anonymous. I will be the founder member and introduce each meeting with the words, 'Hello, my name is Aubrey and I can't stop thinking about Jimmy White'. If other members find themselves in a similar predicament they can ring one another and offer mutual consolation. The treatment will be to deny oneself a tournament a year until the symptoms abate. Full recovery would be reached when one could watch a White match with ranking points at stake without suffering palpitations when Jimmy was in the balls.

Mary wondered aloud if Snookeraholics might have a section for the spouses of failed snooker addicts who foisted all their fantasies on a taciturn cockney who made a career out of failing. She said she'd join up if it came to pass.

For her, the game of snooker was only marginally more interesting than bowls, or watching a plank warp. Her involvement in it was based purely (or impurely) on how Jimmy's results impacted on my mental and, in rare cases involving lampshades, physical well-being. She knew if he lost I could make her life hell as well as my own, so she'd go down on her knees and say prayers to St Anthony that he would win – for both our sakes. She would later go into churches during his matches and offer up secret novenas that he'd come through and win just so as I would be bearable to live with.

I thought sometimes she might have been better off addressing her imprecations to St Jude: the Patron Saint of Hopeless Cases.

Not that Jimmy was hopeless. No, that was me. Hopelessly infatuated with the Whirlwind's fortunes. I had been so ever since I'd witnessed what I still believe to be the most incredible match at Sheffield (yes, the 1985 final included) between Jimmy and Alex Higgins in the 1982 semi-final, when Jimmy so nearly reached the final. He captured the hearts of millions of otherwise sane supporters that day, and captivated many millions more as the soap opera of his life unfolded through various drink-fuelled shenanigans, marital troubles, lurid newspaper headlines and those famous six World Championship final defeats.

But whatever strife visited Jimmy, I was there, shouting for him, willing him on, so deeply involved I felt his pang of pain across my chest as another ball lipped out of the pocket.

His journey was my journey for so much of my life. I was, still am, obsessive. And every single moment of it has thrilled me to my core.

This is the magic of Jimmy White – 'The Whirlwind'.

ZAN'S

IT'S 1976:

In Zan's snooker hall in Tooting, South London a 14-year-old boy called Jimmy White has just made a break of a hundred. He has a pale complexion and an under-fed look. He's wearing a scruffy jumper and jeans and is racing around the table as if this is all too easy. Any time he pots a ball, even the full distance of the table, his expression doesn't change as they slam into the pockets. Casually, he moves swiftly on to the next shot.

When he gets the cue ball where he wants it, around the black spot, he nudges reds gradually away from the pack playing delicate little cannons to dislodge them one by one. The white doesn't travel far, just a few inches here and there as the reds disappear and he's finally down to the colours. When Jimmy pots the brown he does so with a terrific amount of side so that the white ball comes back off the top cushion, at the opposite angle to that which the bemused and startled onlookers expected.

There's a slight whistle from an old man standing by, sipping a can of lager. His name is Bob Davis. Also standing by is a 15-year-old lad called Tony Meo. When Jimmy finishes his break, having cleared the table, Tony racks the balls up again for another frame. This time it's Tony who gets in first. He makes a century too, but it takes him a little more time, and he shows more emotion on the awkward shots.

As they go to set up the balls for a third frame, Davis comes over to Jimmy and says, "Ain't you supposed to be at school, son?"

Jimmy shrugs his shoulders, saying nothing. "We have a day off," Tony says, but Davis doesn't believe him.

"I have an arrangement," Jimmy says, in a smoker's voice.

"How do you mean an arrangement?" Davis asks. "Tony and me, we was in school this morning, that's how it works." Now it's Davis's turn to shrug his shoulders.

Jimmy sits down and lights up a cigarette, smoking it with his thumb and index finger, sucking in those thin cheeks until you feel the nicotine is going all the way down to his toes. "Nice break," says someone from a card table at the other side of the hall and Jimmy breaks into a half-smile, showing a mouthful of crooked teeth.

"How's about you play me for a few quid?" Jimmy shouts across at him.

"No chance," the man replies. "I don't fancy me chances against sharks like you lot."

Jimmy smiles again, as does Tony. Meo is dressed more sharply and wears shoes like spats which makes him look akin to something out of the film *Bugsy Malone*. He has a tan complexion, a Latin look. Outside it's bucketing down. The day darkens but the play goes on, the two young men trading frames without speaking, only moving from the table to notch up their scores or light another cigarette. A small crowd gathers to watch. All you can hear is the gentle clack of the balls and the rain on the roof. If the balls run awkwardly they simply set them up again. They want to pot, pot, pot.

Underneath the table there's a television in a huge binliner, a broken aerial sticking out of the side. Next to the table there are a bunch of watches, all exactly the same, thrown in a heap beside a man dressed in a dirty anorak. Another man with cards in his hands starts arguing figures with him, nodding his head as he makes some kind of deal. A radio crackles in the background. Bob Davis is writing something in a notebook.

Eventually there's a knock on the door and Ted Zanicelli, the owner of the hall, goes out to answer it. "Jimmy White in here?" comes a voice. "Haven't seen him all day," Zanicelli replies. There's a pause. "Mind if I have a look?" the voice says. A face pokes around the door, but all he can see is Tony Meo. Jimmy is under the table.

"Who are you playing with, Tony?" the voice asks.

"Him," Meo replies, pointing to a man at the card table. The man gets up and lazily chalks a cue. He steps up to the table to play a shot.

The feller at the door is unimpressed. "I'll be back later," he harrumphs as he leaves.

After he's gone, Jimmy comes out from under the table and asks, "Who was that?"

"Your brother," Ted says. "Let's see you home after this one."

"All right, guv," says Jimmy, breaking the pack for the last frame of the evening.

Bob Davis has gone to make a phone call. Tony Meo is admiring himself in a mirror, while White is soon on a break, laconic and yet intense, masterfully ordering the balls to do what he wants as a clock on the wall ticks brokenly into the night.

14 years old. Already a snooker prodigy – and already up to no good.

WHIRLWIND

ORDINARY DECENT CRIMINALS

JIMMY WHITE WAS born on 2 May 1962 in a prefab in Balham, south London. He was the youngest of five children. Shortly afterwards the family moved to what he calls "a crap council house with a broken gate".

Jimmy's father, Tommy, suffered from shellshock in the war and was given a medical discharge, which allowed him to meet his future wife, Lily, in a coffee shop in 1943. They spent over a half century together but never married. It wasn't that they didn't love each other; they just never got around to it.

Jimmy had a happy home life, but he hated school and skived off it whenever he could. The baby of the family, he was given a certain amount of free rein, which he grabbed with both hands. He got up to the usual childhood pranks but was shy with girls. Taciturn by nature, whatever wildness was in him expressed itself in action rather than word. As he grew into a teenager, his parents saw little enough of him as he did most of his growing up on the street. That typical south London 1970s youth would inadvertently lead him to discover the infatuation which would change his life.

One day Jimmy was sparring in the street with some other lads when he saw a gang approaching. To dodge the aggressive-looking bunch he ran into a snooker hall – Zan's – run by Ted Zanicelli. The sea of green inside the door entranced him. The colours of the balls on the baize held his attention and the clicks of the balls kissing were music to his ears. It was love at first sight. After that day he was rarely out of the place, learning with a rare hunger in a youngster as he played frame after frame, potting ball after ball.

What's more he was good. Very, very good.

Sometimes things are just meant to happen. Chance occurrences become historical fact. When Elvis Presley was asked what he wanted for his twelfth birthday he said, "A bicycle". But his parents couldn't afford one so they got him a guitar instead. The rest is history. When Jimmy White was asked if he wanted a snooker cue or a racing bike for his twelfth birthday he too asked for the bike. Two days later it was stolen. Shortly afterwards he broke his foot running away from a tube station where he had neglected to pay the fare and ended up with a walking stick. In the absence of a regular cue Jimmy used this stick to play snooker, even managing to notch up a century with it at Ron Gross's club in Neasden, north London, in front of disbelieving onlookers. Among them was 18-year-old Steve Davis. Davis was gobsmacked to see a 12-year-old playing snooker with a walking stick. In his autobiography *Snooker Champion* Davis remarked wryly, 'I must admit there have been a few times since when I've wished he was still playing with it!'

It wasn't just Davis who learned of young Jimmy's prowess early in his fledgling career. Jimmy became friends with another Zan's lover, Tony Meo, aka The Cat. Tony was nearly three years older than Jimmy, but they hit it off and started playing together regularly.

Though born in London, Meo was the son of Italian parents. His Sicilian father died when he was 13 and he was brought up by his mother in the family restaurant in London. His first love was table tennis (at which he also excelled), but when he was bitten by the bug of snooker there was no looking back. Like Jimmy – and so many sports stars, and people of an artistic (if eccentric) disposition – Tony was left-handed. He would soon become the youngest player ever to make a maximum break, which he did against Terry Wittread at the Pot Black Snooker Centre in Clapham aged 17.

Tony and Jimmy wore their school blazers inside out to look inconspicuous in Zan's, but, if anything, such apparel only made their tender ages stick out a mile. They were turfed out by the police whenever they called by, and sometimes by Jimmy's elder brothers or mother, though the latter often slipped him a few quid to go back in after giving him a clip on the ear to publicly show people she cared.

In a later generation Ken Doherty's mother would chase him around his local snooker club in Dublin with a wooden spoon. But both of these women were intrinsically soft. At the back of their minds they knew that children always reverted to doing what they loved best in life no matter how many times they were curbed. Sometimes it was better to turn a blind eye. When his elder brothers dropped in, Jimmy used to run under Table 9, which was in the darkest corner of the club, and wait there till they'd gone.

Tony Meo was a snappy dresser even then: fedora and spats often topped off a black shirt and a white tie. Jimmy brought up the rear in his scruffy jumper and crumpled jeans. The pair dossed around London, dropping in to penny arcades, spending whatever money they had on cigarettes, even pretending they were orphans to cadge food money from sympathetic old dears they met on their travels. They rode the train home without paying, dodging the ticket inspectors because they were usually broke.

It wasn't long before they realised there could be loot – and lots of it – in playing snooker. They started playing money matches together, taking on all-comers, sometimes losing a frame or two to lull their mark into a false sense of security, then cleaning them out. Without knowing it they were the very embodiment of the mantra of Paul Newman's character Eddie Felson in the 1986 film *The Colour of Money*: "Money won is twice as sweet as money earned." Newman's character is a pool hall hustler. Jimmy and Tony were the teenage equivalents in London's snooker halls.

They had their heads screwed on too, often letting their opponents win matches if they felt violence, which often erupted in such venues, was looming. Jimmy tells a chilling story about a 'grass' who was killed by his enemies throwing snooker balls at him one night in a club in Soho after being lured there by a player. Jimmy was determined nothing like that would happen to him. Sometimes he gave people he beat some of their money back so they'd play him again the following day. There was a thrill in winning big sums of money, but a bigger thrill was that of slamming balls into pockets as if there were magnets in them. The problem was the pair blew most of their winnings in various bookies around London. It quickly became addictive. Make money, blow it. Make some more money, blow it again.

Jimmy channelled his wildness into snooker. This was his high, his fix. He reached for his cue the way an alcoholic might reach for a bottle or a junkie for a hypodermic. A different being took over when he was at the table, somebody he probably didn't even recognise himself. On the table the quiet White lad found his voice. This was like a parallel universe to everything else he knew, a womb for dissolutes. Jimmy could imagine himself playing all night and then emerging into the dawn and trying to re-establish himself with the real world. Or was this the real one and everything else an illusion?

At the age of 13, Jimmy went to his father one night and asked him for some money because he wanted to back himself in a game. His father gave him 30 bob. He went down to Zan's with the cash and in no time at all, after winning a string of matches, it became £1,000. That night he staked the whole grand on a match with a local talent in the Streatham Conservative Club and won. So now he had £2,000. According to legend he ironed the crumpled notes that night before showing them to his father. He was hooked.

Quickly, Jimmy swapped school for Zan's on a regular basis, usually being allowed to play for nothing if the place was empty, but when it filled up he had to pay. As he put it himself: "I grew up in the dark." However, he's quick to dispel the notion that he only went to Zan's because he loved snooker. No, initially it was just somewhere to go to get out of the rain, or to escape school. Anything had to be better than that. If Zan's had been a boxing club, maybe Jimmy would have become a boxer. If it had been a gym maybe he'd have become an athlete.

Zan's gave him a love of snooker rather than snooker giving him a love of Zan's. He just needed to escape the dull grind of watching teachers put marks on blackboards and recite boring poetry. As the Eagles put it in the song about his namesake Jimmy Dean, he was 'too cool for school'. He spent so much time in the club that the headmaster at the Ernest Bevin School which he was supposed to be attending, Arthur Beatty, felt something had to be done. He knew Jimmy was good at snooker, and also he knew that forcing the tearaway who was still struggling to read to come to school against his will wasn't going to work.

Beatty didn't understand the full extent of Jimmy's truanting (or snooker prowess) until he read a report of the youngster's first century in Zan's in a local newspaper. Being a lover of the game himself, Beatty chose to use the velvet glove approach to Jimmy rather than the iron fist, trying to tell him that without education he'd never go anywhere in life. Jimmy barely listened. When he saw he was getting nowhere, Beatty offered Jimmy a compromise which would become famous among the Whirlwind's huge fanbase as it grew: Jimmy only need come to school in the mornings. Jimmy jumped at the offer, agreeing gleefully and was sworn to secrecy about his good fortune, but, setting a precedent which would be maintained throughout most of his life, was absent the very next morning. It was a harsh and brutal lesson to Mr Beatty that Jimmy was a lost cause as far as pedagogy was concerned.

Even so, the deal – the first of many eccentric ones the young Tooting lad would make in his life – stood. He got to play and not study. This was bliss for the whizz-kid. No blackboards, no chalk, no copybooks, just the gentle clack of balls disappearing into onion bags as he channelled them to his bidding. In a previous era, the troubleshooting scallywag might have been sent up chimneys or down coalmines to earn a crust, but here at Zan's in the mid-70s, with smoke rings filling the air and East End banter putting an old head on young shoulders, this Artful Dodger found a home from home. While other lads of his age were mucking about on the street, playing five-a-sides or chatting up the local talent, Jimmy preferred to move nimbly around his sward of green, dimly lit by strips of neon. Jimmy grew up thin and pale as the nights shrouded his dank hideaway and he also grew to love the game so much he said "I would have played till my arm fell off."

Jimmy White was blessed to have had someone with the rich spirit of Arthur Beatty to let him have his head. Others weren't so fortunate. John Spencer took up snooker in 1950 at the age of 15 and before the year was out had made his first century, but a report of his prowess in the local paper, the *Bury Times*, caused him to be reprimanded by his teacher, who held to the clichéd belief of the time that the game was the sign of a misspent youth. Spencer didn't hang up his cue directly as a result of this conversation, but it didn't help his motivation. The name of the headmaster, incidentally, was Medler. As Spencer later put it, "Medler by name and Medler by nature."

Spencer then joined the RAF to do his national service and didn't play snooker for the next 11 years. Amazingly after such a lay-off, he managed to take up the game once again, and improve enough to capture three world titles. John Parrott had a similar experience, as he relates in his autobiography *Right On Cue*. Parrott fell in love with a snooker table at first sight, like Jimmy. This caused problems with his PE teacher, who preferred to see him playing football or other more active sports and so put a ban on the green baize. After Parrott won the world championship in 1991, this man had the courtesy to write him a letter with the words, 'How wrong can you be?'

Jimmy never blamed the teachers for his illiteracy. "How could they teach me," he said, "when I wasn't there." He has a point. But from early on in his life Jimmy seemed to have an instinct that he could make it without academic knowledge. In his world of smalltime conmen and would-be spivs, what mattered was one's ability to make split second decisions – and to evade the law. That, he was good at. And his twin abilities – for playing snooker and making money – soon began to draw attention.

It wasn't long before Jimmy and Tony were spotted by Bob Davis, a suspicious-looking man who hung around Zan's and drove a black cab. They called him 'Dodgy Bob'. Davis had watched the young Jimmy, wan of face and slight of build, asserting himself over the sea of green baize as the gentle pock of balls shattered the silence of the otherwise empty hall on midweek days. It didn't take a genius to suss the fact that the boy was a prodigy, such was the effortlessness and speed with which he dispatched the balls into the pockets.

Davis watched mesmerised as, to quote author Gordon Burn in his book *Pocket Money*, 'this scruffy, buck-toothed little kid knocked off century breaks in less time than it took to drive from Clapham Common to the junction.' He realised he was witnessing the birth of greatness at Zan's and one day Davis offered to drive Jimmy and Tony to Ron Gross's club in Neasden to play money matches. The idea was that Bob would get 90 per cent of anything they earned because he would be stumping up the cash for the matches. It was a horrific deal, but the only one anyone was offering them. So the pair agreed – and they blew away all comers. Dodgy Bob lived up to his name. The lads never knew what stakes they were playing for. When they got their measly percentage, even that could have been less than they were entitled to if Davis claimed his stake was less than it actually was.

Soon they got too well known in London circles and Davis started driving them to more far-flung venues. They might almost have been singing 'You've Got to Pick a Pocket or Two' from Lionel Bart's Dickensian musical *Oliver!* as they burned up the miles, the burning lights of low rent emporia puncturing the nights. Jimmy was in love with the uncertainty of it all, the promise of adventure and even danger. He thought to himself: *Maybe I can turn this thing that I do, this thing that comes as natural to me as breathing, into a life.* There would be no more skiving off school, no more hiding under Table 9 when brothers came calling for The Kid. This was legit, or as legit as it got for Dodgy Bob. *With our left hands,* Jimmy thought, *Tony and me can rule the world.*

If Jimmy was the Artful Dodger, Meo was Oliver Twist and Dodgy Bob was Fagin. The two urchins were living the life of people twice their age, getting ferried around London to do something they loved. What was the alternative? Staying in Zan's to play the same people for pin money? 100 per cent of nothing was nothing, so they stuck with it.

Today Dodgy Bob would possibly have been arrested for fraud, if not child abuse and kidnapping, but back in the 1970s it was a more bohemian world and he was allowed free rein with the tearaways. Jimmy often 'came home with the milkman' as he put it, and after sneaking into his house would be tucked up in bed when his mother came in to open the curtains and call him for school, imagining he'd been in his bed all night – or perhaps pretending she didn't know he'd been out gallivanting.

"We never knew where we'd be going next," Jimmy remembers, "tournaments, challenges, anything. If you had £50 then, that was a lot of money, so we used to look after it. Crease it, you know. We just played, getting a few pounds here and there and then suddenly we were wearing suits. It overtook us really. We never thought the game was going to be so big."

Jimmy told Sue Mott in an interview, "Me and Tony, we wasn't illegally bad. We were just hustlers. When I was 13 I could win, like, 300 quid. Enormous amounts. Then all of a sudden you'd walk into a wall, play somebody and he'd beat you and you'd have no money for a couple of months. Not even enough for a cheese roll. I have no idea what I'd have become without snooker. I never had a chance to be a thief or anything, but I was in that environment. A couple of me schoolfriends turned out not too good. Bad boys. I only knew one thing: I'd never have got a job. Certainly not."

Jimmy never left people in any doubt that the relationships he forged during these picaresque days were the ones closest to his heart. "It was villains I used to know," he says, "villains and thieves to tell the truth, but they were good to me. They never harmed their own." These were ODCs, Ordinary Decent Criminals. They obeyed their own code.

But the admirers of his talents weren't restricted to those who would make money out of him. When Jimmy was still 13 he had met Maureen Mockler, a friend of Meo's. Maureen liked Jimmy's slapdash personality, but was less enamoured of his dress sense, or lack of it. Jimmy found himself asking the older Meo for a loan of his shoes for his first date with Maureen. Tony said no, even though he had almost as many pairs as Imelda Marcos. Jimmy put his fist through a window in a rush of anger at being refused and began their stormy relationship by going dancing with Maureen with blood gushing out of him.

For a couple of years or so, Maureen stayed in the background as Jimmy and Tony hit the road. "At 15 we was earning fortunes," Jimmy said, "earning money we couldn't count. We'd travel everywhere and anywhere to play the club champion. Because he'd been cleaning up in the local league, all his mates would back him and we just cleaned up. That went on for about three years until everyone got wise to us. I used to hand me mum 90 per cent of the pile and go off gambling with the rest."

Maureen didn't mind roughing it with Jimmy. They were like a hand-me-down Hansel and Gretel, an inner-city Romeo and Juliet. She didn't expect flowers and roses on their dates; blue cue-tip chalkdust and smoke would have been more likely. But they clicked, two latterday hippies freewheeling their way through a subculture of promise and danger, a catchpenny twist of possibilities where you didn't ask too many questions and lived for the moment.

After he got close to Maureen, she became a replacement for Tony, who, by 1979, had legitimised himself amidst the professional ranks in a sport which was increasingly popular on television thanks to the likes of Ray Reardon and Alex Higgins. Now it was Maureen who was delegated to look after the money, always ready to beat a hasty retreat when Jimmy gave her the signal. "We were like Bonnie and Clyde," is the way Jimmy puts it, "only we weren't robbing banks. We were just having fun together."

WHIRLWIND

JIMMY WHITE'S FIRST real manager was a man called Henry West, who also looked after Patsy Fagan, Ireland's best-known snooker player before Alex Higgins. Fagan was the resident professional at the Ron Gross Snooker Centre in Neasden when Jimmy first met him. He reached the final of the English Amateur Championship in 1975 and two years later won UK Championship.

Fagan was dogged for much of his career by the 'yips', a terrible affliction that spreads from the mind to the hands, which, seemingly uncontrollably, fail to deliver the cue in the direction of the white ball successfully, screwing it so it misses the object ball badly enough to fail to pot it. It's a condition which has little medical explanation and which can visit its sufferers without a second's notice. It's ended many a top player's career and it can also haunt golfers, making them unable to let go of the club smoothly, causing them to yank the ball wide of their intended target. Fagan consulted psychiatrists and hypnotists to try and cure it, losing many ranking points until it suddenly, without explanation, disappeared. It took three years, and a lot of money, for Fagan to get his potting arm back. Many years later the yips would afflict Jimmy, but that was in the future.

There was a potential explanation for Fagan, though. He was involved in a bad car accident in 1977 and took to the bottle afterwards. Many of the muscles in his right arm were damaged, which is a major problem for any right-handed snooker player. The year afterwards, in a match with Fred Davis at Sheffield, Fagan developed a phobia with the rest. It was then he sought the help of a hypnotist.

West was a man who could sell sand to the Arabs, as John Hennessy once said. He made his fortune by installing a stash of pool tables in bars – without being asked to – and dumping the existing ones. He spotted Jimmy's potential early and took him under his wing, away from the extortionate cab driver. At least West channelled Jimmy's talent towards making a 'proper' career out of the game, rather than on skimming a minimum of 90 per cent off his earnings.

With West pulling the strings, Jimmy progressed with the kind of speed which matched the frantic pace of his play and was earning him the nickname 'Whirlwind'. Aged 14, in 1976 Jimmy had won the Pontin's Junior tournament. A photograph of him receiving the winner's cheque from Sir Fred Pontin shows him as a cherubic lad with a deep fringe across his starry eyes. The suit he's wearing is a size too big. The knot on his tie looks to be as big as the tie itself. By the following year, 1977, aged 15, he had 50 centuries to his credit. That was the year he came into national prominence by becoming the youngest player ever to be selected for the London team that won the Inter Counties Championship.

That season he also won the National Under-16 Snooker Championship, beating Dave Bonney in the final, and also the National Under-16 title. He continued his startling progress by becoming the youngest English Amateur Champion in history two years later when he beat Dave Martin 13-10 in a tiny hall in Helston, Cornwall where 600 people sat huddled together to watch the prodigy. There wasn't even room for Jimmy's mother. Instead she stood outside practically eating cigarettes to calm herself. (So now we know where her son got it from.) Jimmy was just a month shy of his 17th birthday.

Life was less plain sailing, however, off the green baize. Drink got a grip on Jimmy from a young age. He has never denied this or kept it a secret. How could he? The stories associated with his incessant boozing are legion and many have passed into folklore. Those famous tales begin around the time when he was playing for England at the Home International Amateur Series in 1980 and he joined his friend Joe O'Boye for a session on the sauce. Incredibly, Jimmy managed to compile a break of 59 while still feeling the after-effects of this, but then fell to the floor drunk at the feet of his perplexed opponent, Steve Newbury. Having lost the match 3-0 to Newbury, Jimmy stumbled back to his chalet and decided to have a bath. Worried about what his errant prodigy was up to, West went in search of White and discovered him in the tub accompanied by his cue. Jerking his arm back and forth, Jimmy declared, in a drunken slur, "I'm going to paddle to Tasmania." He meant it too.

By this time the party-loving lads were gaining something of a reputation. O'Boye went on to win the English Amateur Championship that year, but had his application for professional status rejected three successive times in the next three years, largely due to his fondness for the bottle and the antics which that led him to. Barry Hearn famously opined that the only thing that could save Joe was "a brain transplant".

The Home International Amateur Series series was a prelude to the World Amateur Championships, which were due to be held in Tasmania. Jimmy had been selected to represent England, but the Newbury debacle threatened that. After some tense negotiations, he was eventually given a slap on the wrist and a fine of £200, but was allowed to travel to Tasmania.

The fine hardly made White mend his ways. After he reached his destination he continued to be the Jimmy you just couldn't tie down. On the way from the airport to the hotel, he stopped off at a racetrack and blew his total allowance for the trip of £1,500 on horses and booze. "If there had been a race for dead donkeys," he said afterwards, "I would have put a bet on it."

£1,500 was a huge amount of money for the authorities to have entrusted to a youngster who was so clearly incapable of coping with it burning a hole in his pocket. But they did and the inevitable happened. The problem Jimmy had now was he faced a fortnight with not a penny to his name. In a strange kind of way, the fact that he couldn't go out on a regular basis, couldn't gamble and couldn't drink was the making of Jimmy Down Under as he focused on what he was actually there for. He lived on the breadline for the duration of the tournament, but still managed to gain revenge on Steve Newbury in the quarter-final and Paul Mifsud in the semi-final. He annihilated Australia's Ron Atkins 11-2 in the final to become World Amateur Champion.

It was in incredible achievement for a street urchin of just 18 years and 191 days – all the more so when one considers that he played Atkins with a ferocious hangover, the result of a 'celebration party' he held the night before at which his 'guests' supplied all the booze (although in time such an abundance of pre-match bravado would come to haunt him).

This called for a proper celebration. On the way home, Jimmy stopped off in Calcutta, picking up the Indian Championship in transit – as you would. When he got back to England he found his pro ticket waiting for him.

Everything looked to be rosy, but Jimmy's life was starting to become complicated. Maureen fell pregnant and there was a lot of friction between the White and Mockler families as to who was 'responsible'. This was, of course, back in the days when children born out of wedlock were still considered controversial and shameful.

As a single mother-to-be Maureen was given a small flat in a high rise in Battersea by the council, but she found being tied down so tightly by motherhood was boring, not least because Jimmy was away – partying – so much. Even when he was at 'home', he never seemed to know where he was going to hang his hat. Their relationship was as unpredictable as his game. They fell out, sometimes violently, with both inflicting scratches on the other, often utterly inadvertently, although it would be the mental scars which would be the most difficult to recover from. Jimmy ended up spending as much time at his parents' house or on friends' floors as he did in Battersea.

When their child was born they called her Lauren. Jimmy and Maureen still fought like cats and dogs, living together and then apart, going home to their respective families when the pressure got too much. Maureen berated Jimmy for the amount of time he was spending in places she referred to as "seedy dives". For his part Jimmy admitted he was fazed by his sudden celebrity status. "I started to get recognised," he told Richard Green of the *Observer*, "and I wasn't prepared for it. I was having a great time in bars and nightclubs. At that age it's hard to see where it all leads."

Mostly, to the pub, bookies or snooker hall.

When Lauren was 16 months old, Jimmy and Maureen got on well enough for long enough to decide they wanted to get married, although the decision didn't carry too much conviction. They booked a registry office but didn't tell anyone in case they had one of their barnstorming rows before the day in question, which might result in a cancellation. The set date was 28 March. Maureen said, not totally in jest, that maybe they should move it forward a few days to April Fools' Day because their whole relationship was like an April Fools' joke.

The marriage went ahead all right, but without too many trimmings. Both families were done out of their 'Big Day', and neither was too chuffed when told of the union. That simply caused more friction between the pair and Maureen told Jimmy she was thinking of having the marriage annulled even before their wedding day was out. Jimmy slept at his family home that night. "I think someone gave us a wedding present," he remembers, vaguely. Hardly the greatest day of their lives and it made little difference to their day-to-day existence. The pair of them continued to live as they had before their nuptials, without all the commitment the institution of marriage entailed. Jimmy hankered after the Tony Meo/Dodgy Bob days, in which he had to scarper out of venues like the Paul Newman character from *The Hustler* for fear of having his thumbs broken by some disgruntled pundit.

"Nowadays," he said in an interview, almost with a tinge of regret, "you can win and nobody's going to run off with the cheque." Prosperity, to be sure, had its price. You couldn't go from fame to obscurity the way you went from obscurity to fame. Stardom was a one-way trip. Jimmy reluctantly had to accept that Zan's was a thing of the past, as was ragamuffin Jimmy with his 'paid on Friday, broke on Monday, kiss me at the end of the pier' lifestyle.

Already Jimmy White was faced with a crossroads in his life. His emotions were all over the place. He was high on the adventure of it all but didn't have much of an idea where he was headed, if anywhere. "My head was in a jamjar," was the way he later put it. Thrust into an adult world before he'd properly got out of his childhood one, Jimmy had an old head on young shoulders in streetwise terms, but in so many other ways he was totally unequipped to deal with the buzz.

Being introduced to the professional circuit meant Jimmy came into regular contact with his hero, Alex 'Hurricane' Higgins, the man who influenced his style of play more than any other. He had first encountered Higgins in 1975 at Pontins holiday camp where Higgins was playing an exhibition match. Jimmy was there with Tony Meo as usual, hanging around Higgins's caravan, hoping to meet the 1972 World Champion, whose life had been a succession of booze-induced scandals and brilliant victories ever since. When Higgins came out and started throwing breadcrumbs at the seagulls, Jimmy said, in that inimitable cockney screech of his, "Oi, Mister, what the 'ell are you doing wiv those shitehawks?" Higgins restrained himself from laughing and replied that he was getting his killer instinct going so he could win an exhibition match later that day. All Jimmy heard was the word 'kill', so he scarpered. He was 13 at the time.

In 1980, Jimmy played an exhibition match against Higgins in which he actually took a frame off him. Higgins then asked Jimmy's father if the youngster would accompany him on the exhibition tour. Jimmy was over the moon that his idol would want him on board. Maureen, not surprisingly, wasn't too keen on him hanging out with Higgins. She knew it meant even more irresponsibility for her husband, and even more alcohol. She was right.

In fact Maureen didn't ever worry about Jimmy being with other women as much as other men. She wasn't a WAG who imagined him in some five star hotel with a starlet, but rather in some dingy dive slurping up pints of bitter with deadbeat hangers-on who would waylay him and exploit his 'in for a penny, in for a pound' personality. She always knew that in life as well as on the table Jimmy could resist everything except temptation.

Jimmy later told Sue Mott of the *Sunday Times*, "I'm very lucky to have Maureen (considering) the amount of times I used to go missing. Mind you, she knew where I was. I wasn't having affairs or anything. I was basically getting drunk with the boys." Even as a teenager, he'd told another interviewer, he was more interested in playing snooker than chasing skirt. "Tony Knowles has a bit of a following," he joked, "but I get all the donkeys after me."

Life with Maureen continued to be eccentric. They lived a kind of raffish existence as the career of the Boy Wonder developed in fits and starts. She wasn't at all domesticated, but this didn't remotely bother Jimmy as he liked fast food, and eating out. He envisaged a kind of 'married single life' with her, as if things would continue as they had been during their courtship. To be fair to him, Jimmy didn't want her to be the 'little lady sitting at home' as he went out on the town

He wanted her to enjoy herself too. He wasn't prepared to stay in and babysit while she did so, however. If they had their rows – and they were blazing ones – that was okay by him. It came with the package.

He knew he needed to be rapped on the knuckles when he'd been a bad boy and in a perverse kind of way he almost craved punishment if he'd earned it. Like Higgins he expected to be locked out of the house some nights, or to have to sleep on the sofa. He knew actions had consequences. If you did the crime you had to do the time. Like the L'Oreal girl, Maureen was worth it. Fire and brimstone was followed by periods of peace. But as the children (four girls; Lauren, Ashleigh, Georgia and Breeze) began arriving in their marriage the pressures mounted up.

Sometimes when Maureen locked Jimmy out, he roared in at her and woke the neighbours. Or else he went down to the local telephone kiosk and rang her. There was also a night where the two of them got too physical with one another and ended up being taken to two separate hospitals to be treated for their wounds. Maureen didn't press charges on this occasion. She knew Jimmy wasn't violent by nature, and that sometimes she gave as good as she got when it came to a brouhaha between them. And of course she loved him – even if they couldn't live together. Jimmy didn't press charges either. How could he? He loved her.

"During one argument," Jimmy said, putting his hands up, "I jumped all over Maureen's car, up and down like a trampoline, banging and battering it with a dustbin lid." Afterwards he went out and bought her another car. He was always contrite and she generally forgave him, within reason.

He relished his status as World Amateur Champion. It was a supreme achievement. His thoughts turned to his future in the game. He wanted Geoff Lomas, the owner of a snooker club in Manchester who he'd grown to trust, to manage him. Lomas was handling Higgins, which was a full-time job, so he asked Harvey Lisberg, the owner of Kennedy Street Enterprises, to come in on the deal. The pair of them bought Jimmy from West for £10,000 and allied him to a new company they'd just set up called Sportsworld. World semi-finalists John Virgo and David Taylor had already been signed up here.

Lomas was a man of many parts. A former bookie and computer firm director, he also ran a cosmetic surgery company. He even sold vibrating armchairs to arthritis sufferers. Like Jimmy, Lomas needed new challenges all the while to stimulate him. He found one in snooker, which was just blossoming into a very high profile mainstream sport. Lisberg was coming to the game from a different place, having managed the pop groups 10CC and Herman's Hermits.

Lisberg gained Jimmy's confidence early on by promising him appearance money at events even if he lost in the first round. As somebody who had managed high profile bands, Lisberg found it disgraceful that a performer of any kind might have nothing financial to show for an event, even an event where one didn't perform well. Sadly, the WPBSA knocked this on the head, but Jimmy appreciated the gesture.

To prepare him for his new glam lifestyle, Sportsworld immediately gave Jimmy a makeover, rubbing off the rough edges by enticing him to 'dress posh', have his teeth straightened and his hair curled. Jimmy hardly recognised himself afterwards. He wasn't accustomed to the necessity of having an image to play the game he loved. Nobody had looked at the way he dressed in Zan's as he honed his skills not so many years before. Nobody wore Savile Row suits there. Jimmy joked that you wiped your shoes coming out of that establishment rather than going in. So he wasn't too keen on his new guise.

Jimmy preferred jeans to a suit and didn't take too kindly to having to preen like a toff for cameras. Somehow, it didn't sit well with someone who'd been born in a prefab. He started wearing French shirts, though, and an earring. Things had moved on a bit since he'd approached Tony Meo for some clobber for that first date with Maureen.

Jimmy wasn't big on fame. It was a distraction from what he did. Agents and managers were other distractions. They got in the way of the movement of his hand along the cloth, the brain power it took to craft an awkward clearance. That's why he did runners when people told him to be in places – or *not* be in places. Responsibility was death to his young mind. He preferred to run with the slick crowd, the Flash Harrys. If there was a scene at a club, he was in. Set 'em up again, bartender, and let the devil take the hindmost. We'll be dead long enough.

Jean Rafferty in her book *The Cruel Game* said Jimmy had his image laundered to match his surname. The real Jimmy, she suggested, would be happier playing in some half-lit hall in the middle of nowhere than in the Crucible or the Hexagon. It was true that he was losing a connection with his past. He wore the robes of his trade, but nobody could own his soul. He still gave the impression he was most at home in a bookie's office with a pencil behind his ear as he laid down a few quid on the nags.

Lomas knew you could dress him up but you couldn't tie Jimmy down. "As soon as your back was turned," he moaned, "the tie would be off and the jacket chucked under a table somewhere." It was like putting Huckleberry Finn into a tuxedo and expecting him to go dining instead of fishing.

In the opinion of John Virgo, "Most of us have to feel completely comfortable with what we're wearing before we can give our best. Not so Jimmy. I've seen him turn up at a tournament without a dress suit, go out and buy one, take the pins out and put it straight on. Then splash on some after-shave, spilling it all down the front of the new suit, and go straight out and play an absolute blinder."

With his background in the music business, Lisberg referred to snooker as "the pop music of the 80s . And who better to spearhead the boom than a man who personified all the street cred of any popstar worth their salt? He brought a rock star buzz to snooker management, increasing the profile and thus the earnings of his stable. He knew Jimmy was media gold as long as he could keep him out of the headlines for the wrong reasons. (Like Higgins, his off-the-table antics were seized upon by the gossip press who thrived on such salacious titbits.) Lisberg wanted to keep Jimmy on the back pages of such newspapers rather than the front, Higgins having cornered the market at both ends over the previous decade. One Alex Higgins was enough for anyone in a lifetime, Lisberg felt. So Jimmy was on media probation until he got a few more years on the clock.

Like others, Lisberg worried about Jimmy, although for selfish reasons. Because White played and lived like Higgins, many managers had been initially wary of him. Higgins, everyone knew, had 'previous' with managers. He let them down, failing to turn up for gigs as well as having punch-ups and hellacious nights on the town. Jimmy looked quieter, but you never knew. There could be a cauldron in there waiting to explode. As the saying went, the quiet ones were often the worst.

Lisberg was right. A succession of incidents followed. First, Jimmy was arrested for looting in Brixton shortly after being signed to Sportsworld, which caused some head-rolling for all concerned. He was celebrating his recent marriage to Maureen at the time the Brixton riots broke out and, ignited by the spontaneity for which he was to become famous, he saw a handbag in an already-broken shop window and started clowning around with it. When Jimmy heard police approaching he ran off with the handbag still around his shoulder. He was charged – ludicrously, it seems now – with larceny, which didn't bode well for his future standing in the game. Lomas was outraged, feeling his prize jewel was already showing signs of being more trouble than he was worth. But did the police have nothing better to do than nab a potential handbag-snatcher considering the carnage that was unfolding around them?

Jimmy was also thrown out of a hotel around this time after the manager objected to him ordering eight breakfasts one morning when the room had been booked for one. You can appreciate the manager's point of view. Not even Bill Werbeniuk, snooker's portly Canadian star, could eat eight breakfasts. But as Jimmy pointed out, his seven friends hadn't been using the room to sleep in. They were up all night playing cards. Neither did the manager come to him privately and express his dissatisfaction with him ordering the eight breakfasts, as he should have done, opting instead to write a letter, which predictably got leaked to newspapers, thereby furthering Lisberg's headaches with Jimmy.

Given what he knew about him when he took Jimmy on, Lisberg could hardly expect him to be lily white, but the manager knew it was incumbent on him to rein the pupil in a bit and protect him from the kind of people who seemed to seek him out and drag him down to their level. Maybe, he thought, he even needed to protect Jimmy from himself.

After a few other embarrassing incidents became a critical mass, Lomas decided to write an open letter to a newspaper about Jimmy to try to make him see he was living his life wrongly. Jimmy saw the irony in this – bizarrely Lisberg was paying good money to kill stories while Lomas was busy dishing the dirt to the same editors.

Amidst all this mayhem, Jimmy had a career on the professional circuit to get off the ground. To any snooker player the holy grail is the World Championship, held at the Crucible Theatre in Sheffield each spring. Jimmy was no different in this and fought like a tiger to reach the televised latter stages by defeating Jim Meadowcroft in a tough match in the final qualifying round, edging him out by the narrowest of margins, 9-8. In the first round of those 1981 World Championships, Jimmy was narrowly beaten 10-8 by Steve Davis, the man who would become his nemesis right through this decade. Davis took a 4-0 lead, but the Whirlwind began to grow his reputation to the watching millions by fighting back to 7-8 and then 8-9 before the more experienced man won out. After disposing of Jimmy, Davis went on to win his first World Championship that year, seeing off Higgins, Terry Griffiths, Cliff Thorburn and Doug Mountjoy on the way.

It was a tough draw for Jimmy. Davis had already won the Coral Championship, beating Higgins 16-6 in the final, having thrashed Terry Griffiths 9-0 in the semis. Davis had also beaten Jimmy 7-3 in the Pontins Open in 1979, and 6-5 in the Louth Pro-Am in 1980, but Jimmy had one victory over Davis to his credit, beating him 5-3 in the Demmy Pro-Am final in Manchester.

Davis's manager Barry Hearn almost threw the 24-year-old across the table in jubilation as the last ball went down. A new era in snooker had dawned, but for some it would spell the death knell of adventurousness. Jimmy, in any case, pushed Davis harder than anyone else that year at Sheffield, beginning a classic sporting rivalry which would enthrall viewers for well over a decade. The Whirlwind's flair versus 'Interesting' Davis's dour tactical approach. It divided the nation. If you supported Jimmy you were for the underdog, for skill, for ability over doggedness, for adventure over monotony. If you supported Davis you were for grinding safety play, the triumph of dogma over panache; you preferred accumulation over style.

The narrow defeat to the man who become world champion spurred Jimmy on and he won his first professional tournament, the Langs Scottish Masters, in Glasgow in 1981, beating three world champions – Ray Reardon, Davis and Cliff Thorburn – along the way.

Jimmy had a summons for the looting incident hanging over his head during this tournament. In fact there was even a question he might not be able to play in the final. Maybe that galvanised him – especially against ex-policeman Reardon, if not Steve Davis. Jimmy was too shy to make a speech after the last ball was potted. It would have been the first time he was approached to do anything vaguely approaching PR and he was thrown. Losing finalist Thorburn was asked if he could fill in the blanks, but he put it back on Jimmy. It was, after all, his night. Eventually Jimmy mumbled, "I'd like to thank Langs whiskey for a lovely evening." That was it. It was hardly a novel, but the job had been done. He was a title-holder. Just as importantly, he pocketed a cool £8,000 for his week's work.

It was a massive achievement for a 19-year-old and made him the youngest winner of a major ranking tournament in the history of the game. Being the youngest English Amateur Champion and youngest World Amateur Champion as well made this the icing on the cake. It seemed he was doing everything younger than everyone else. In the modern era players mature in the game at a far younger age, but Jimmy was unique in this for his time as he was unique in so many other ways.

Davis was peeved to have his winning streak broken by the pretender to his crown. "I'm greedy," admitted Mr Consistency. "I'd win the Grand National, the Boat Race and the Cup final all in the same year if I could." Higgins often said Davis didn't care about how he played if it got him the silverware. Most players are like that to an extent, but Davis took the lust for winning to another level.

Jimmy followed that up with a further tournament victory, this time in the Northern Ireland Classic. He scored another win over Thorburn in the first round, then beat Doug Mountjoy 9-8 in a thrilling semi-final, but the best part was coming from 9-7 down in the final to beat Davis 11-9.

It was after this tournament that Jimmy had committed his first professional public PR gaffe when he said that Davis was "just another player". It was a comment Jimmy would come to rue as he faced Davis in the next tournament on the calendar, the Coral UK Championship. Jimmy took out Clive Everton, John Virgo, Ray Reardon and Dennis Taylor – a lot of big scalps – en route to the semi-finals and looked good to go all the way, but the wounded Davis annihilated him 9-0 in the semi-final before going on to take the title.

It was the first major trouncing of Jimmy's life and it knocked the wind out of his sails, giving him something of a psychological block over Davis that would last throughout most of his career. It led to Jimmy dubbing Davis 'The Nugget'; the toughest player in the game to beat. Not many people would find issue with that appraisal over the course of the decade that was just beginning.

Jimmy's comment after the Northern Ireland final was beefed up by *The Sun* newspaper before the Coral UK encounter to ratchet up the pre-match tension and rivalry. With typical tabloid bluster, they claimed Jimmy had said far more derogatory things about Davis than he actually had, which only served to make

Davis more psyched up for the match. This also put more pressure on Jimmy to, as he put it, "deliver". It was a lot to ask for a young man just making inroads into the pro game.

As Davis was at the table, Jimmy looked like the proverbial rabbit caught in the headlights. He clearly wanted to be somewhere else. The first four frames could have gone either way, but after that he was pummelled mercilessly. He sat in his chair for long periods as Davis potted incessantly, looking even younger than his tender years, awaiting the inevitable whitewash. "I was lucky to get nil," he quipped afterwards.

But Jimmy White was now a name, a face on the circuit, a feared opponent, a title-winner. He also was garnering a growing number of supporters of his flash image and flair play, particularly through his incredible ability to pot seemingly impossible balls.

Jimmy loved the attention. He once told an interviewer, "When I'm out there and see a tasty looking shot, I can't refuse it. Sometimes I try something chancey and it doesn't come off, but when it does it's the biggest buzz of all. When I go for a completely mad shot and it slams into the pocket that's unbeatable. The crowd go completely nuts and I know I've done something that will give them a bit to talk about when they're driving home."

Over the course of the next year or so, he fought gamely on the circuit with mixed results. He bowed out 5-2 to Eddie Charlton in the first round of the 1982 Benson & Hedges Masters. In the Tolly Cobbold Classic, he ousted Mark Wildman in the qualifying stages before decisively knocking out Cliff Thorburn and Perrie Mans in the first and second rounds respectively. Kirk Stevens provided a sterner test in the quarter-finals, but Jimmy took that match 13-9 before losing in the semi-finals as Dennis Taylor beat him 3-1.

He failed to retain his Langs Masters title in 1982, going out by the odd frame to Taylor in the opening round. He lost in the second round of the Jameson Open to Cliff Wilson, but reached the final of the Professional Players Tournament where Reardon beat him 10-5. Jimmy got his revenge on Wilson in the second round of the Coral UK that year, but again fell to Reardon in the quarter-finals, albeit by the narrowest of margins at 9-8. He then reached the semi-finals of the Hofmeister World Doubles with Tony Knowles, but was knocked out by Davis and old friend Tony Meo.

Success, failure, success, failure. The pattern was beginning...

WHIRLWIND

THE WHIRLWIND MEETS
THE HURRICANE

THERE ARE MANY great friendships which cross the competitive divide in sporting history. Andrew Flintoff and Brett Lee in cricket, Pelé and Gordon Banks in football and Steve Ovett and Seb Coe in athletics. Warriors in battle all, but able to raise a drink and a cheer off the field of play. But the camaraderie which was struck up between Alex Higgins and Jimmy White, the two waifs and strays of the snooker world, was remarkable even when measured against these cross-border alliances.

White was the Jimmy Dean to Higgins's Brando. In the words of Montgomery Clift, if Brando said, "Fuck you," Dean said, "Help me".

He was the Sancho Panza to Higgins's Don Quixote, the man who could get into a ruck with you but then escape ... just about. Jimmy did Alex's bidding and enjoyed the wild ride, but when Alex tipped himself over the edge Jimmy held back, as if this was a bridge too far even for him.

Even so, Jimmy, like most hot-blooded young men, needed his highs. Snooker was one of them. Drink was another and smoking a third. And then there was the danger of the unknown, the feeling he got when he took on a risky red – or a dangerous venue. These were all buzzes. He didn't look tortured, like Alex, or act tortured, like Alex, but inside himself he had an energy that needed an outlet.

But he saw an extension of himself in Alex. Higgins brought out his worst side and his best side, the parts of himself he hardly knew existed, the parts he both loved and hated, curbed and indulged. Together they made sweet music on the baize, even if it often ended on a discordant note. Alex was like a voice inside Jimmy that said, *thus far and no further*. He was Jimmy's alter ego, the man he could have been if he was more outgoing but was better not to be because introversion gave him the discipline the rest of him lacked.

Alex brought Jimmy a step closer to the precipice of life than Tony Meo ever could. He was his idol, but a dangerous one. He put down the roadblocks Jimmy had to sidestep to eventually outgrow Higgins, and also realise the dreams Alex planted inside his febrile head.

They first met in serious competition in the biggest tournament of all, the 1982 World Championships. Jimmy was looking to improve upon his first round exit the previous season, while Higgins was still trying to recapture the form that had seen him win the title at the first attempt in 1972, only to fall foul of a life of booze and bouts of anger thereafter.

First round matches are often the graveyards of favourites. This had been the case for Steve Davis in his attempt to retain the world championship. He slumped to a shock 10-2 defeat against Tony Knowles. Davis was unsettled going into the match, the whirligig of being world champion weighing heavily on his shoulders. He was also promoting a book, which cut into his practice time. Knowles got off to a good start, which meant Davis was always on the back foot, unusual for him. Knowles didn't have to do anything sensational to beat him, just keep the pressure on. Before Davis knew what was happening he was out of the tournament in round one. Another first-time winner had failed to retain the title.

Terry Griffiths became the new favourite but he was knocked out by Willie Thorne. The draw was opening up, which favoured players like Higgins and Jimmy. It's a pity they were on a collision course to meet in the semi-final.

Many people still say this was the best match ever played at the Crucible. I'm one of them. Forget the 1985 final. Sure, that had the nation gripped. It was good, even great, but this match had everything. It produced such a magnificent quality of snooker that most viewers wondered if they weren't, in effect, watching the final. Jimmy, like the Higgins of a decade before, was chasing a place in the history books because he was still only 19 years old, which would have made him an even younger winner than Higgins had been in 1972. Old timer Ray Reardon was waiting for the winner in the final. Everyone knew that whoever won this tussle would take 'Dracula' out.

Higgins had been regarded as a spent force before the tournament. It was ten years since he'd won it and that decade had garnered more headlines for his obstreperousness than his occasional brilliance at the table. A fortnight before the championship he had been dropped by Harvey Lisberg – needless to say the manager would regret the decision sorely – who'd had enough of his antics. Higgins was also having problems with his wife Lauren.

The match got off to a rattling start, the lead changing often, amid big breaks and little safety play. Both players smoked and drank during it, accentuating the nervous tension round the table. Higgins raced into a 4-1 lead, but Jimmy pulled level after the first session, going to his dressing-room the happier man, walking off to a standing ovation following his rousing comeback. According to a press report of the time, Higgins cried in his dressing room because the crowd were behind Jimmy. It was the first time the Hurricane had ever lost the public vote. Higgins was also upset he'd lost the sixth frame, which he'd had at his mercy before his concentration was disturbed by the click of a camera. The lead changed often after this, each man trading punch and counter-punch as Higgins tried to tether the young lion.

Jimmy won one of his frames in less than three minutes. In a way he looked like he was out-Higginsing Higgins, beating him at the kind of game Higgins had birthed. Crash, bang, wallop – have some of that! But Higgins dug in and kept in touch.

What amazed me about Jimmy – it was my first time seeing him play – was his laconic style, the way he could pot balls almost as soon as look at them. His innate feel for how to build the break and the quickness of his thinking around the table were startling. Higgins was a dramatist, but Jimmy seemed almost embarrassed by his own talent. He didn't seem to line shots up, to study them for those few seconds every other player took before drawing back the cue and striking. Having decided to play a particular ball, there seemed no doubt in his mind that it wouldn't drop. This would have been understandable if the ball was hanging on the jaws of the pocket, but some of these were length-of-the-table shots. It was incredible.

He looked even younger than his years. His under-nourished cheeks stood out like golf balls. His eyes were frightened. He seemed to have a Beatle haircut, the jet-black sheen setting the pallor of his face into high relief. He was almost like something from a Rembrandt painting.

In his chair Jimmy looked bewildered by the whole situation. He might have have been an orphan child, might even have been on the point of tears. But when he came to the table a new being appeared to take over, a new spirit breathed into his body suddenly, a spirit that was almost seismic. He moved round the arena like a predator and suddenly the forlorn, doom-laden face of a moment ago disappeared as he sprang to seize his chance amid a clattering of balls into pockets. He cued very low on the white and didn't move it around much, staying near the black spot, dislodging a red here and there from the pack as each break rose to 20 and then 30. There was a fluency in his play that made each shot almost an extension of the last one rather than a separate entity. Another thing I noticed was that he brought the white into the cluster of reds when potting a red, as opposed to the average player who only went into the cluster when playing a colour. There was only one other player who was noted for doing this, and that was Alex Higgins. Were we watching a new Higgins?

For ten years I'd watched the Hurricane, followed him through all of the highs and all of the lows, lived through his agonies and ecstasies, knowing that this was where it was at, that the way Alex Higgins played snooker was the way to play snooker. Was it possible that what Higgins had done for the game was now about to be emulated? Was it possible that it could, whisper it, be transcended?

A few moments later Jimmy missed what was a relatively simple pot and I thought this was also something Higgins often did, either through lack of concentration or boredom, as if the easy shots didn't pose the kind of challenge the hard ones did.

Higgins started off the match trying to outpot Jimmy, but when he twigged this wasn't working, he started to, as he says himself, box clever, to tie the pretender to the throne up in knots. Here was Higgins the poacher-turned-gamekeeper, doing to Jimmy what John Spencer had tried to do to him exactly ten years before when he'd won the world title against all the odds. The Irishman was pulling out every strategic ruse he could dream up, resisting any urge to play the kind of shot that had given him his soubriquet, taking everything as it came in the tight frames without any heroics, making desperate attempts to slow down the pace of a player who didn't seem to know what safety was, nor care less. Higgins had once had this wildness, he too had salivated with this relentless lust. Ten years in the desert, however, had somewhat diluted his aggressiveness.

He fed off Jimmy's freneticism, cannibalising it like a vulture, continuing to recharge his batteries as he walked the knife-edge between success and failure, fight and flight. Jimmy, on the contrary, was being affected by his own form of nerves, which showed in that pale, almost tubercular face.

Jimmy led 8-7, 11-8 and 15-13. The target was 16. Higgins pulled him back to 15-14, but Jimmy still only needed one more frame. He built up a 59 lead in the next. Would it be decisive?

Higgins captured the way he was feeling at this moment in his autobiography, *From The Eye of the Hurricane*: 'This youngster whom I loved like a brother was making me work like a dog. I needed this frame to stay in the contest, and the one after it for a place in the final. The adrenalin was pumping, but I wasn't feeling the strain. Those money games that I'd been playing over the previous fifteen years stood me in good stead.'

The pressure was beginning to tell on Jimmy. He knew he only needed a few more balls, but also that he had everything to lose if he slipped up. While playing a shot with the rest – in years to come he would frequently be extolled as the best rest player in the world – he missed a red into the top right-hand corner. Now the ball was in Higgins' court. Could he play with it?

Janice Hale wrote: 'Before the final session, Higgins opened the Bible at the Acts of the Apostles. For the last two frames of the match he had a small gold Sacred Heart in his mouth, sent by a well-wisher in Dublin. None of the millions watching on TV could have guessed that the man who put their hearts in their mouths was experiencing just that himself in such a tangible way.'

Amidst incredible tension inside the Crucible arena, and at home in millions of living rooms, Higgins got down to business, potting solidly and steadily. All of the balls were out of position. It had to be a break carved out of piecemeal shots. He was making it all up as he went along, perhaps more surprised than anyone else that he was still at the table as he got down to the last six balls. What little colour there ever was seemed to have drained from Jimmy's face as he watched Higgins pot yellow, green, brown, blue, pink and black to take the frame. It was a body blow that would take Jimmy a long time to recover from. Maybe forever. For the first time but not the last, he was about to snatch defeat from the jaws of victory.

Probably the most astounding shot of the break came when Higgins used sidespin and buckets of left-hand side on the white when he was playing the blue off its spot into the green pocket while the white was near the pink spot. The idea was to get the white back there for one of the loose reds. His snooker brain was in overdrive. Even if he missed, the next red wasn't a 'gimme', so he wasn't putting all his eggs in one basket.

With his nostrils flaring like the jockey he once was and his body jerking every which way – not just before his shots but during them – Higgins did everything the rule books said not to, but the balls still went in so who could criticise him?

This was how Alex described his near-impossible clearance: 'Jimmy only needed one colour to win, but left the red too close to the pink and missed it. I knew that was my chance, but if I strayed a fraction out of line it was all over. There was so much pressure on me, I finished up in no man's land with the cue ball in a hopeless position. The temptation was to play safe, but with four or five reds on the table it would have been skating on thin ice. The tension was crackling, but I had that tunnel vision with the lamp of victory burning at the end of it. I was getting outside help – a combination of the man upstairs and Lauren.'

Higgins claimed the break was inspired by Muhammad Ali's fight against George Foreman in 1974. Ronnie O'Sullivan, aged six, was transfixed watching it on television. Years later he said, "I think it's the most stupid clearance I've ever seen in my life." It was certainly unorthodox. Each shot seemed to be a holding one, half pot and half safety. The canny gambler was backing everything each way just in case he missed. But he didn't. Ted Lowe put it another way: "Every shot was a trick shot."

With the match squared at 15-15, Higgins looked home and dry. He put his index finger up to the crowd as if to say 'Only one more to win', as he stalked back to his seat to mop his brow in preparation for the do or die decider. He was looking forward to the final frame because, as he wrote, 'Jimmy hadn't played for a good 15 to 20 minutes and I was just off the table, feeling good, confident and full of the flow of play.'

This was prophetic because as things worked out, Jimmy made little or no impression on the last frame. He was, as they say in the trade, 'gone'. It had been the 30th frame that killed him off, not the 31st. "I was almost sorry I'd beaten him," Higgins said. "I couldn't just shake his hand. I had to hug him as if to say, 'Sorry babe but you'll have your day'."

Of course, what neither of them knew then was that he actually wouldn't – at least in Sheffield.

Jimmy knew it was the penultimate frame that won the day for Alex. He said of that 69 break: "The balls were spread so awkwardly I didn't believe he could dish up, but Alex pulled off the best clearance of his life to pip me on the black."

Higgins felt sorry for his victim: "I'll not forget the sight of Jimmy walking out of the arena. He'd played magnificent snooker, scented victory, tasted it even, and had it dashed from his lips at the last moment. When you see so much talent in such a young player and know that if it hadn't been for one slip he'd have been on top of the world your heart goes out to him. But he took defeat well. We became soulmates afterwards."

Perhaps aptly given what was to follow, it was in this defeat that the nation fell in love with Jimmy White. It was a love affair which would be as tortuous as any of the other relationships in Jimmy's life, but a gloriously warm one, all the same.

I'd mixed reactions myself. I'd been a huge fan of Higgins for so long and when he came to the table I was entranced. Like most people I empathised with all the pain he showed. He gave snooker to the people because he represented them. He showed how much it meant to him to win, and how much it hurt to lose.

But I also fell for Jimmy right from the off in that match. He too was a man of the people, a man who would eventually wrestle Higgins's title of People's Champion away from him. It was Jimmy's vulnerability that endeared him to the nation. He was the conduit for a thousand longings among the stay-at-home housewives in hidden England, the people who went to the Job Centre and then came home and ate muffins. They saw something in Jimmy that they recognised, a raw look like you got in actors like Tom Courtenay or Alan Bates. They watched him and identified with his inarticulate longing. It was a feeling that grew and grew over more than a decade. But it started at that moment.

Alex spoke of Jimmy in glowing terms: "Jimmy and I are the only ones who play snooker for love. We each have a hundred shots in our armoury. No-one else comes near that. Jimmy doesn't like hanging around any more than I do. He has the power game. It's great for the public and it makes such a change from the rest of the snails on the circuit. People watch snooker to see balls going down. The faster the better. Jimmy and I believed in potting as fast as possible and getting on with the next frame. I know for a fact that we both played for century breaks. We weren't interested in fifties."

Jimmy was equally in awe of Higgins, saying, "He's the only player other players will actually go and watch. Including me. They might not admit it, but players will sneak to venues to see Alex."

But although there were so many similarities between the two, Jimmy was different. He was more of an introvert than Higgins. He didn't seek to be a party animal. He was the kind of man-boy you wanted to hug. But his style of play came from Higgins. It was the style of a man who didn't know when to stop. He always went for one shot too many and paid the price. That was the charm of Jimmy. You knew you'd prefer to watch him lose than any other player win.

The main difference between Jimmy and Higgins was in the way they carried themselves. One exploded and the other imploded. Higgins pulled off the impossible and said, 'Look, no hands'. When Jimmy did something dynamic he looked as if he wanted to disappear under the floorboards. But if you looked hard enough you could see he was pleased with himself.

If Jimmy was an actor he would have been a method actor. If he was a poet he would have been a lyricist. Higgins would have written an epic. (Steve Davis would probably have gravitated towards the sonnet.) Anyone who ever lost a frame or a dame found a kindred spirit in Higgins. He put snooker on the map – but then he proceeded to vomit over that map.

Geoff Lomas brought some reality to proceedings when he said, "I'm glad Jimmy got beat. He would have killed himself if he won. He's even over the top now. Anyway, you can't call yourself world champion unless you beat Davis along the way."

Buoyed up by the Jimmy victory – and an undisclosed amount of vodka – Higgins played superb snooker in the final against Reardon. He led 15-12 at one point, but the Welshman fought back to 15-15. Higgins then stepped up a gear and went 17-15 ahead. He had just one more frame to win and he did it in style, making a total clearance of 135. Reardon, who had six world titles to his credit but would never win another one, was gutted. Higgins summoned his wife and child into the arena and broke down in tears. It was like the last scene of a Hollywood melodrama as he gushed, reaching his hands out pleadingly for his family to come to him, embracing his wife and cradling his daughter in his arms. Here was the 'Rocky' of the green baize.

Asked to explain the secret of his success, Alex cooed, "I had the ten-year itch." It was as simple as that. "Now I can die happy," he told the crowd. He'd had a well documented rivalry with Reardon over the years and this seemed to put a seal on it. Most of the viewers had been rooting for the Ulster man. The flawed genius had beaten the six times world champion.

Much later, Reardon said of Alex, "He uses running side, reverse side, back side, any sort of side. The only side he hasn't attempted is suicide." In actual fact Higgins had, as he documented in his book *Through the Looking Glass*. In 1983 Davis annihilated him 16-5 in the semi-finals in Sheffield. Higgins went into a depression as a result and tried to kill himself while on holiday in Majorca with his wife Lynn. He narrowly escaped death after slipping into a coma. The honeymoon of the victory over Jimmy hadn't lasted long.

But for now Higgins had submerged his demons, even if only temporarily. The night was his. After the final was over he drank like there was no tomorrow. He'd proved his doubters wrong and conquered his old enemy.

Before the tournament Higgins had been all but written off by the press. Now he was back from the dead, Lazarus had taken the scalp of Dracula in no mean fashion. Neither had Jimmy any regrets. After he recovered from the initial disappointment he joked he was "delirious for the bastard".

From then on they would not often be found apart. Their third bedfellow would almost always be trouble.

After winning the world title, Alex was approached by a promoter to do a series of exhibitions around Northern Ireland while showing off the trophy to fans. He asked Jimmy if he'd like to accompany him. Jimmy was delighted to have the opportunity. The pair of them travelled round the country in a makeshift tour bus that had a small cooker and toilet, but stayed in hotels when they reached their destinations. On the fourth day of the tour the promoter disappeared with the money and the driver refused to drive them anywhere because he hadn't been paid. In fact he even refused to talk to them, locking himself inside the bus – with the World Championship trophy as hostage.

Jimmy stood outside the bus pleading with him to come out, but the driver refused. They couldn't leave him because their cues were in there, and of course the trophy. "I'm holding onto your gear until I'm paid," he shouted out at Jimmy. "The law is on my side."

"Open the bloody door," Alex screeched back animatedly. "We haven't been paid either."

"Bollocks," the driver replied.

Alex phoned 999 and after a while a policeman arrived on a pushbike. When the promoter still refused to come out, Higgins said to the policeman, "I'll shoot him. Someone get me a gun. That'll be the easiest thing." By this stage Jimmy was creased up in laughter.

This all took place in Londonderry, in a particularly difficult time during the Troubles. By now a large number of the town's residents had gathered, and even a television crew. It was turning into a circus. The policeman cautioned, "Now Alex, you can't threaten to shoot him."

"Look, he's got food and drink in there, and a toilet. He can hold out for a month," Jimmy pointed out. "Let's see what he'll take."

By this time the army had arrived, heavily armed, imagining it was some kind of sectarian threat. Alex and Jimmy clubbed together and offered the driver £250 to come out. He finally emerged from the bus with the gear and they made off to their next gig. But they never tracked down the promoter.

Jimmy and Alex were destined to become bosom buddies after those intense shared experiences. Because of the friendship, Jimmy played many exhibitions in rural areas of Ireland that were organised by his friends Con and Richie Dunne, a pair of twins who liked a good time. "We would drive into the middle of absolutely nowhere," Jimmy remembers with some nostalgia, "remote little villages where the hotels had pigs, soda bread, stout, ruddy complexions and two beds stuck together for a bridal suite." And, needless to say, a pub.

Con was a snooker promoter from Dublin and Richie was the national Irish coach, but the *craic* was their priority. Jimmy often stayed with the Dunnes, but he also spent time in hotels and bedsits or cheap and cheerful B&Bs. Once he even stayed with Phil Lynott, the lead singer from Thin Lizzy, who was to die tragically from drugs.

The actor Richard Harris liked to tell a story about leaving his London home to go out for a packet of cigarettes and ending up in Ireland for a month. Jimmy had similar experiences. Because of his laidback personality and his love of mischief, particularly drink-fuelled mischief, it was little surprise that Ireland's eccentricities would hold an added appeal for him. The Irish took him to their heart in a special way, almost like an adoptive son, and when he won the Irish Masters in 1985 it seemed to copper-fasten his devotion to the Emerald Isle.

The two Dunne brothers ran a ferry service from Dublin Airport to various hotels they owned throughout Ireland, and also held the franchise from the Irish Pool Billiards and Snooker Association to bring snooker players from the airport to Goffs in their courtesy buses. Such journeys were adventurous, to say the least, and always involved drink, singing and, quite frequently, police attention.

Jimmy also played many exhibition matches with Higgins in Ireland during this time. It was at one of these, in the National Stadium, that I first got his autograph. They were incredible matches, both players going for everything and potting balls, as they say, from the lightbulbs. It was hard to know who to root for, the local hero or the cockney firebrand. It was a pity there had to be a loser in these tussles, but then nobody ever really lost an exhibition match except the player who bored you and these two certainly didn't. They took their lead from one another, playing ridiculous positional shots off two and three cushions which somehow turned out right. It was snooker from the gods and audiences responded with lots of foot-stamping, hand-waving and even standing ovations. The post-match celebrations would also be equally raucous. The Whirlwind and the Hurricane were truly a lethal cocktail.

One night Jimmy was with Alex when Higgins became enraged at a group of press photographers camped outside his door. He tried to throw his TV set out of the window, but it was made of leaded glass so it bounced back, hitting him on the chest and knocking him flying. Jimmy was paralytic with laughter. According to Jimmy, Higgins could pick a fight with his own shadow. And he loved him because of this.

Higgins was so often the impish instigator of trouble between Jimmy and his wife, Maureen. Like Jimmy, Higgins has a daughter called Lauren. He once asked Maureen, while he was staying at Jimmy's house, to change her daughter's name to avoid the duplication. Maureen was livid as her Lauren had been born before the Higgins child. Alex refused to acknowledge this, indulging in a bout of Creative Mathematics.

In the Higgins ambience, which Jimmy fully embraced, players frequently smoked and drank alcohol during matches. Many tournaments were sponsored by tobacco companies. That has changed, changed utterly in the modern game. Players now sip water and smoke, if at all, behind closed doors. Before matches they're in the gym rather than the ginmill. In mid-session intervals they're often at the practice table instead of receiving intravenous injections of Arthur Guinness.

The stories of Jimmy and Alex's escapades are legion. In his autobiography Higgins tells a funny story of a night out boozing with Jimmy and Jimmy's friend Pee Wee, this time in England. At the end of the night they called for a taxi, but the landlord of the pub they were drinking in, which was in the heart of the countryside, told them there were no taxis in that neck of the woods. He suggested they walk, but walking was never one of Jimmy's favourite hobbies. "Sod that," he said, "if the other drinkers in the pub can drive home pissed, so can I."

The theory might have been good, but it was a rainy night and soon afterwards the car left the road, going up a steep bank before smashing into a brick wall. Alex went through the windscreen but miraculously was unhurt. The other two were wearing their seatbelts and suffered only minor injuries. Alex walked back to a bewildered Jimmy and said, "I am like a cat, James. I have nine lives and I think I have just used one of them up." Jimmy replied, "Get in the car, you mad bastard. We've got to get away before the old bill get here."

They drove to Jimmy's house but as soon as they got the car into the garage, like a classic episode of *Only Fools and Horses*, the engine fell out onto the floor. All they could do was laugh. They went into the house and drinks were poured all around as they bathed their wounds. Then Jimmy sobered up he said, "Oh Christ, the bloody windscreen is still up there on the wall."

"So what?" Higgins replied, "it's no good now. The car's a fucking write-off."

"I know that, you muppet," Jimmy said, "but the bleeding tax disc has the registration number on it. When the old bill finds that I'll get nicked."

He decided to go back for it, so rang a taxi firm and had them drive him to the scene of the accident and then back home with it. Safely home, he was challenged to a game of snooker by the now jubilant Higgins for 300 quid. Jimmy wasn't in for any levity and grabbed the cue from Higgins's hand, flinging it across the room, after which he threw Higgins out ot the house. Alex wasn't having any of this, so he went to a neighbour's house and told him that Jimmy White had assaulted him and that he wanted him to call the police to have him arrested. The man took pity on him and invited him in for a cup of tea. Higgins sat up with him all night. At 5am he even prevailed upon him to drive him a hundred miles to Reading, where he had an exhibition match scheduled. This, he said, had been his plan all along!

Higgins tells another story about a time he and Jimmy were in a small town in Ireland and decided to put on a number of bets. Higgins wrote the bets on horses out wrongly and Jimmy blew a fuse, but when they watched the first race on a pub television, the outsider Higgins had mistakenly gambled on romped home. The pair of them did an Irish jig to celebrate.

Later on another one of the outsiders Higgins had accidentally put a bet on also won, so they ended up over 2,500 punts to the good. When they got back to the bookies, to their dismay they saw a sign saying 'No bets over 100 punts will be paid'.

Realising they'd been done, they sought out the bookie and found out he'd hightailed it to the local golf course. They made their way there and faced him down.

"Give us our fucking money," demanded Higgins, "or I'll use you for a 7 iron."

"Yeah, cough up, you conning old git," Jimmy added. With that the bookie emptied a wad of notes from his pocket and they went home happy, having enjoyed one of their most profitable days ever as gamblers. And all because of a Higgins oversight.

SNOOKER LOOPY

IN 1983, AFTER the depressed Alex Higgins tried to kill himself while on holiday, dark days revisited the Hurricane, which appeared to have blown itself out.

But where the Hurricane's force dwindled, the Whirlwind's was becoming a raging torrent – occasionally devastating and merciless. Mind you, at other times Jimmy's lack of maturity could show through. As good as his stunning victories were, he was perfectly capable of also going on to lose to the likes of Cliff Wilson or Joe Johnson. Jimmy's form could go up and down like a fiddler's elbow. He seemed to be a loose cannon in many of the tournaments he participated in, the literal wild card. He often fought a rearguard action which meant he was chasing the game from the outset. When he got in front he relaxed, but maybe too much. He didn't have the killer instinct, didn't twist the knife. His casual safety play hadn't been a problem when he'd been on the amateur circuit, but in the top flight of the game every white that didn't reach the baulk cushion – sometimes it stopped even above the blue spot – could result in heavy scoring from his opponent. Pretty soon the word got out that this was how to trap him. If you had patience you could outwit the precocious *wunderkind*.

Jimmy's prolific scoring was where his game shone. He became one of the first players to play shots into the centre pocket that were at oblique (or even blind) angles, and to pot them with alarming frequency. He also liked very thin cuts, some of which didn't even look 'on' to the untutored eye. When these went in he had little control over where the cue ball was going, but he was a good enough potter for that not to matter too much. He also became exemplary at fizzing the cue ball round the table, often with reverse side, to cannon into the pack and create a frame-winning opportunity from almost nothing. This was something he learned from Higgins, who was often accused of catapulting the white off extra cushions for theatrical effect, or applying side to it even when it wasn't needed – in contrast with, say, someone like 'Steady' Eddie Charlton, who, the joke went, only *pretended* to use side.

Where Jimmy tended to come a cropper was when he was playing an important pot along the cushion. These were headaches to any player, but particular agonies to this man. Other players could comfortably refuse such shots, electing for a safety instead, or even a snooker. Such negativity wasn't really an option when you were the Whirlwind.

When I first started watching Jimmy I was teaching in a small primary school in the north of Dublin and playing snooker in the evening time in the Dublin leagues. I wasn't overly good at either activity. Sometimes I wrote articles about him for the papers – I felt that was where my life was headed – so I found myself watching him more and more on television. As I watched him lining up a shot I'd play it with him, my hand trying to guide the cue through the line. It was like being in a car with a learner driver, putting your foot down on an imaginary brake if you felt they were going too fast. But there was no way you could put brakes on Jimmy. Like ol' Blue Eyes, Jimmy was going to do it His Way. Maybe that's why managers despaired of him.

He was at his mercurial best in patches, but then the old demons would kick in and he fell over fences nobody expected. It was as if he grew bored after negotiating the main hurdles and dropped his concentration for the lower ones. It was the challenge Jimmy loved: moving reds off cushions, developing awkward colours, working around situations where he had to take low value colours with reds because the higher ones were tied up. And then when everything returned to normal he'd miss an easy one and let his opponent in to take advantage of all the hard work he'd done getting the colours back on their spots. It was heartbreaking to watch for anyone who saw him as Britain's favourite son, the darling of the housewives – and a fair few househusbands too.

Jimmy didn't always compose himself in the heat of battle. He could be distracted by noise from an adjoining table, an untelegraphed roar from the crowd, even Auntie Mavis in the front row unwrapping a sweet paper, God bless her. Other players took time-outs to have a sip of water (or beer) during awkward breaks so they could assess the situation, but Jimmy wanted to do it all in one go, playing as if his house was on fire, or as if he had to pay for the lights. Head down and go.

American author Erica Jong has a saying: 'If you don't risk anything, you risk even more.' The epithet applied to Jimmy's career, for better and for worse. Often he created something out of nothing by his attacking style, but often too he made problems where there weren't any. In this he could be likened to the talismanic golfer of the time Seve Ballesteros, who was renowned for his fantastic escapes from self-created problems. This was the tightrope Jimmy walked, and why many of his matches, indeed frames, carried the aura of convoluted thrillers. Nobody, least of all himself, knew what twists and turns lay ahead as he changed his gameplan to root out misplaced reds and colours. The audience erupted when he had his 'eureka' experiences, but put their heads in their hands when he carried them up blind alleys or painted himself into corners. Like a masochist, he went where angels feared to tread. Like sadists, we followed every step of the way. He played with fire and burned his hands. We followed suit.

When Jimmy played an elder statesman of the game like Ray Reardon it was like a son looking for a father's commendation. I remember watching a frame between them in the early 1980s where it all hinged on the black; a delicate cut into the middle pocket. Reardon wouldn't have taken it on because it was at a blind angle. Jimmy did, and got it. That was a seminal moment for me, the moment where the son took over from the father.

Conversely, Jimmy's own father was like a son to him. Tommy White looked up to Jimmy as if he was fulfilling the dreams he himself had nurtured in the war years. He idolised him on and off the table. Jimmy sucked this up as he sucked everything up in life, hungering for the next thrill.

In some matches Jimmy looked rough, as if he'd got out of the wrong side of the bed that morning, or maybe hadn't been to bed at all. He was never a morning person at the best of times, but you always had the feeling that he might just be playing solely on the remaining adrenalin left over from a night on the tiles. The bow tie, untied and draped around his neck at times gave credence to this theory.

This was perhaps the only thing he had in common with Ray 'Dracula' Reardon. He was a nocturnal animal. The later the match, the better Jimmy seemed to play. The longer it went on, the more he seemed to have in the tank. In the mornings he didn't seem to care much. His eyes looked dead and his concentration was non-existent. You got the impression he could have been thinking more about the Tia Maria he left behind at Stringfellows the night before rather than the stun and run-through he had to play to develop the blue.

Harvey Lisberg urged Jimmy to adopt a more scientific approach to things, to concentrate on what he was doing as well as developing more stringent preparation patterns. But Jimmy couldn't think like that. He played each shot as he felt it, unwilling to apply different tactics for different players. Many players playing Jimmy accentuated their safety play, trying to trap him into mistakes, but Jimmy didn't believe in doing the like by them. He preferred to play the table rather than the player. "It doesn't matter who I play" was a frequent mantra in pre-match interviews. But maybe if he'd used some psychology Jimmy would have gone farther in more tournaments, even allowing for the bacchanalian life he was living off the table.

It helped that Jimmy's rise to fame coincided with the emergence of the game into popular culture. Or was it the other way round? Whichever, Ray Reardon said in 1983, "There's too much money in it now. We're in a world of agents and managers. All the fun's gone out of it." One takes his point, but he wouldn't have refused the money if his star was on the rise that year – or indeed turned away the agents and managers.

Jimmy never had much to say to interviewers. He preferred to let his snooker do the talking. He had a nice line in banter, but usually you could gauge more from the way he was feeling by his facial expressions and/or grimaces than anything that came out of his mouth. He frequently told pressmen that he was playing well in practice, as if this was somehow supposed to translate to the table. The reason it couldn't was that there was a safety net in practice play. There were no consequences if you missed. In practice there wasn't a lot of difference between the world Number 1 and, say, the world 21, but when players got in front of the television cameras under the hot lights and the pressure kicked in, that was where you separated the men from the boys.

By now this infuriating genius had become a captivating personality on and off the table. He made the game look so easy it was uncanny. You had to play it to know it wasn't. By this time I'd been playing it myself for nearly 20 years and still found it difficult to make a 30 break. Jimmy knocked in the balls almost without looking at them. He must have inspired many people to take up a cue – and then put it down again soon afterwards in frustration. I was one of those inspired fans, so when Jimmy came to Ireland in 1983 to play in the Benson & Hedges Masters in Goffs Sales Ring in Co. Kildare I tried to meet him. I was with my brother Hugo. When we arrived at Goffs we were informed Jimmy was at the Keadeen Hotel in Newbridge with his manager Gary Miller-Cheevers. I drove to Newbridge, despite having consumed a fair amount of drink by this time. When I got to the hotel I made an overture to Miller-Cheevers, telling him I wanted to interview Jimmy for an article I was doing on him. Thanks but no thanks came the reply.

I was so distraught I couldn't think straight. I was also pretty drunk, having been on the sauce for most of the day in anticipation of finally getting to talk to Jimmy. Hugo told me I should get a taxi home and come back for the car the next day. That was never going to happen. I stormed into the driver's seat and told him he was welcome to come with me or hitch-hike back to Dublin. As soon as I got on the motorway I felt my vision being impaired. The windscreen looked foggy. Cars were travelling at a ferocious speed and I accelerated to match them. Hugo was screaming at me to slow down, but I wouldn't listen. He tried to wrench the steering wheel from me, but I wouldn't let go. A part of me didn't care if I crashed. I hardly knew who I was by now, never mind who Jimmy White was. I knew Hugo was right, that I had to get off the motorway. I indicated left, trying to get onto the hard shoulder, just when a small black car tried to pass me on the blind side. By some miracle I braked to avoid it and we were thrown forward. The car seemed to find its own way to the closest ditch. After it came to rest, I felt a bump on my head, but that was all. Hugo sat there stunned. There was nothing either of us could say. Suddenly I felt sober from the fright. I got out of the car and walked up and down the road.

It was beginning to rain, but I almost welcomed it. I thought of the song 'Raining In My Heart'. When I got back into the car I was fairly drenched. I wasn't sure it would start when I turned the ignition, but it did. Hugo was just shaking his head. It was as if he'd given up on me, as if he didn't care either. "He's just a snooker player," he shouted at me.

In a way I felt the evening wasn't about Jimmy any more, but about my need to carry through anything I started. I went into a rant to Hugo about how he was backing out on me just as we got close to the main target. I said I felt Jimmy would be kindly disposed to me if only I could get close to him.

At this point Hugo exploded. "I'm not travelling with you any more," he said, "if you don't shut up. Your obsession with Jimmy White is unhealthy. It's extreme."

It was the wrong thing to say to me in my condition. I told him I was thinking of turning the car around and going back to Kildare. "If you do that," he said, "you'll kill one person, not two, because I'm getting out."

I just kept driving, in the opposite direction to where I wanted to be, my head whirling. I can't remember arriving home.

The next morning Hugo came round and said to me casually, "Don't worry, you'll get him next year." That was all it meant to him. He didn't understand I was on the point of suicide at being spurned.

In the weeks following I made many frantic calls to England, locking myself in a room to make the calls so no-one would know. If I'm honest, my desire to meet Jimmy was becoming like an obsession with a rock star, or even a woman. Was it love or lust?

Whichever, my failure to succeed drove me on to try and set up a meeting with him, this time through official channels and less fuelled by drink. There were very friendly secretaries on the line and they all promised to give him my messages, but he never got back to me – ever the elusive Pimpernel. At one point I thought I'd made the breakthrough when his secretary told me she was setting up a match between Jimmy and myself in one of his London haunts where I could do a fly-on-the-wall interview with him as we played a frame or two. Crushingly, that never happened either. In fact I never got to talk to Jimmy once in all of that time.

Later in the year Jimmy came to Dublin to play an exhibition in the National Stadium with Higgins as his sparring partner. Again my loyalties were divided. It was a classic match, but Higgins totally dominated the last half of it. Nonetheless, there was only one player I wanted to speak to when it was over. This was the first time I shook his hand, the first time I saw him close up, the first time I got his autograph. After the match was over I lined up in a queue about nine deep as Jimmy sat behind a desk signing posters of himself. When I got to the head of the queue I wanted to tell him how much he meant to me, wanted to tell him he played snooker like I'd always wanted to play it, that every time I watched him he made my tongue stick to the roof of my mouth. I wanted to say all this and much more, but as Jimmy White sat before me all that came out was, "Could you sign this for me?"

And he put his spidery left-handed scrawl on my picture of himself and looked up for the next person in line.

* * *

1983 began badly for Jimmy. Now 21, he needed to be emerging through the pack of newcomers to the game and making his case for being one of the most feared opponents in the land. Instead, he was surprisingly beaten by David Taylor in the opening round of the Lada Classic and then Higgins defeated him in the quarter-finals of the Benson & Hedges Irish Masters. After his great showing in the World Championships the previous year, Jimmy was dismissed in the first round in Sheffield 10-8 to his old friend Tony Meo. Higgins knocked him out of the Langs Masters. Was he a flash in the pan after all?

Jimmy fared better at the Coral UK, reaching the semi-finals where Steve Davis beat him comprehensively, before going 7-0 up on Higgins in the final and proceeding to lose 16-15 in one of the most dramatic finishes to a snooker match ever seen. But then there was further disappointment for Jimmy as Davis and Meo crushed him and partner Tony Knowles 10-2 in the Hofmeister Doubles final.

Although he wasn't yet making his mark in terms of winning tournaments, a burgeoning rivalry was developing with the man from Romford; one which was to become as keen and competitive as White's friendship with Higgins was loving and explosive. Davis beat Jimmy again in the 1984 Langs Scottish Masters final, as if to rub salt into the wound, but Jimmy won the Carlsberg trophy in Ireland to boost his morale. This was only a four man event, but his 9-7 victory over Tony Knowles in the final produced some great snooker. Davis, who else, knocked Jimmy out of the Coral UK Open at the quarter-final stage.

Kirk Stevens, the man in the ice cream suit, made a 147 against Jimmy in the 1984 Benson & Hedges Masters semi-final at Wembley. Jimmy was leading 5-3 when Stevens made his maximum. One might have expected Jimmy's concentration to be disturbed by it, but it often works the other way. Dazed by his own brilliance, Stevens made no impression on the next frame, which Jimmy won with a century to take the match. Stevens congratulated him warmly, satisfied with having made a little bit of history (it was only the fourth 147 in tournament play at the time) even though he was now out of the competition. After the match David Vine asked Jimmy if he saw any similarity between the Stevens match and the one he played with Higgins at the same stage two years before. "Yeah," Jimmy replied with characteristic bluntness, "but I won this one." And winning was becoming an increasing habit for Jimmy, although he still continued to do dangerous things along the way. There's a shot from that match which is so good it's still to be found on the internet for posterity to enjoy: Jimmy screws off a pink in stupendous fashion to rest perfectly in position to finish the frame.

After beating Stevens, Jimmy went on to defeat Terry Griffiths in the final of the Masters, thereby pocketing the fattest pay cheque of his career thus far. Geoff Lomas claimed part of the credit for the victory, telling Jimmy's mother that it was his open letter to the paper regarding Jimmy's casualness that finally made him see sense.

It just got better and better in 1984 as Jimmy partnered Higgins to win the Hofmeister World Doubles. Davis and Tony Meo were going for a hat-trick that year but they were kicked into touch by the Whirlwind and the Hurricane in the semi-final. They hammered Cliff Thorburn and Willie Thorne 10-2 in the final.

With an array of victories behind his blossoming talent, Jimmy also looked good value for a world title in 1984. At Sheffield he put out stalwarts like Rex Williams, Eddie Charlton and Cliff Thorburn before a heart-stopping semi-final with Kirk Stevens that went on late into the night. Stevens led 12-10 going into the last session, but lost the match 16-14.

This was Jimmy's first Great Escape at Sheffield and something I should point out as all too often the emphasis is placed on his defeats in the final. It was a match he could easily have lost as Stevens was on fire, but Jimmy rose to the challenge with the kind of fighting spirit that electrified his fans. He won and in superb fashion. Was Jimmy White about to fulfil his destiny and become world champion?

I remember going out for a long walk after this match to clear my head. The relief was palpable. Jimmy was brilliant, but you never knew where you stood with him. It was always like a bonus when he won, no matter who he was playing. He made you work for it. It was part of the magnetism which drew me in

The final was classic chalk and cheese as Jimmy was to face the man quickly becoming his nemesis, Steve Davis. The Nugget was hungrier than ever, having won the tournament the previous year after the Knowles humiliation of '82. Would he become the first player of the modern game to retain the title? The hype and expectation was the greatest for a final yet. By now Davis was already something of an institution in the game. A man who rarely missed (if he gave you one chance in a frame, that was usually about it) he was, however, snooker's equivalent of the Queen. His soubriquet was 'Interesting' and he was indeed that to talk to, but on the table he was anything but. His tussle with Jimmy was billed as the duel between Apollo and Dionysius. The Adrenophile versus the Somnambulist.

Davis was a publicist's dream in the sense that he had a squeaky clean lifestyle and gave all the right soundbites in interviews. But instead of his straightforward, percentage game making him unpopular, Davis was almost as heralded as Jimmy himself. In fact Davis was the most watched sportsman in all of Britain in 1983.

In his autobiography, Davis reveals that he modelled his style on the Joe Davis manual, a book he calls the Bible. 'Every time Dad and I played together,' he tells us, 'he made sure I kept to the book. And there was never any scoring. Just coaching, coaching all the time. Dad reckoned that trying to score points could be a distraction. He was obsessed with technique. It was the basis of my game. All I did for three years was learn, learn, learn. Grafting hard, with Dad insisting that I should be close to perfection all the time in all I did. Some lads of my age might have found the hours of practice tediously repetitive, but I lapped up every minute of it, and would have welcomed more.'

The antithesis of Jimmy White's approach.

Davis was aware of how hot Jimmy was, but that only fired him up more. He loved silencing the crowd by his devastating potting whenever he played Higgins (whom he had a good record against) and looked forward to doing the same to Jimmy. He knew many people found him dull, but neither did that faze him. "I let the balls do the talking," he said.

Davis's father Bill wasn't thrown by the hype surrounding Jimmy. "They say Steve is boring to watch," he said, "but that's because he plays snooker. He pots the ball with the minimum of effort and gets the white ball in position for the next shot. Higgins or White will do the same thing but they'll run it along the rail, side-screw it off the lampshade and make it do a figure eight. The audience goes bananas for that stuff, but they do the same thing in the end." Maybe it depended on whether one saw snooker as an exhibition sport or not. The White/Higgins approach was fraught with danger so merited more brownie points on the Richter scale of bravery – at least as far as I was concerned.

In the first session of the final, Davis raced into an astounding 7-1 lead almost before Jimmy knew the match was on. Clearly he was feeling the after-effects of the marathon with Stevens the night before. He was also trying to push the boat out too much. The contrast in styles was palpable, but it was also bringing astoundingly different results. Davis did the simple things well, whereas Jimmy tried to pull rabbits from hats. But of course that left something to error. The higher the climb the bigger the drop. When Jimmy started to play you sensed the electricity in the audience, as if anything could explode from that powder keg. But then Davis stepped in like a bomb disposal expert.

Davis domesticated the game while Jimmy defamiliarised it. Davis was happiest when the colours were on their spots and the pack tight. Jimmy seemed more content with the principle of chaos theory. He got an extra buzz when things ran ragged, when he had to contrive unorthodox solutions to problems, or pot his way out of trouble. If Davis was a computer, it had to be deprogrammed by the youngster.

At 7-1 down that prospect looked unlikely. Most viewers expected another anti-climactic final like the one of the previous year where Davis trounced Cliff Thorburn 18-6. Davis stood at 12-4 after the day's play ended without having done anything really sensational. There was really only one player in the match. "I don't win matches by blasting players off the table," Davis admitted. "I prefer to numb them into submission. My style of play is based on Ray Reardon. He'd slowly strangle you to death like a boa constrictor. I do that too." If snooker hadn't been invented, I thought, looking at Davis, he would probably have been an accountant. Jimmy would have been a maverick gambler.

The following day, Jimmy had nothing to lose, so, according to White's law of entropy, his risk-taking started to pay off. He threw everything at Davis but the kitchen sink and Davis started to reel from the pummelling. By the end of the next session Jimmy had clawed his way back to just 13-11 down, winning the session 7-1. Game on. But could he continue the incredible fightback in the evening? The whirlwind was in the eye of a storm.

The match turned on a shot Davis played in the first frame of the final evening session. Jimmy was leading by 34 points and looking like closing the gap to just one frame, but Davis potted a red and dislodged another red that was on the cushion as well as a 'safe' blue. Jimmy didn't get back to the table. Davis had taken a risk, as Jimmy did so often, and got lucky. You can't predict what will happen in situations like that. His main priority had been to pot the red, but it worked out perfectly and he won the frame. The score was now 14-11 and soon Davis went 15-11 ahead. The four-frame lead looked unassailable.

Again Jimmy fought back gamely, winning four out of the next five frames to pull up to just one frame behind at 16-15. His charge continued and he led by 55 points to 32 in the 32nd frame with just the colours left. But Davis snatched the frame on the black to go 17-15 up. Any one of the six colours would have allowed Jimmy to level the match.

Other players would have crumbled under the pressure, but Jimmy returned the favour in the next frame, stealing it on the last ball. 17-16 to Davis. It could hardly get more dramatic than this. Davis needed one, Jimmy two. Could the unthinkable happen?

Jimmy looked set to win the next frame too, but on a break of 40 he left the cue ball too close to the pink and had to play away. As it happened, he wasn't to pot another ball in the frame (or match), Davis closing him out by 77 points to 40. Another mistake was taking on a long green towards the end of the frame. He missed it by a wide margin. It was a frustrated shot from a frustrated player and it sealed his fate in the match. One can look back on shots like this, or the one he missed against Higgins in 1982 in the 30th frame, and ask why and how. But we should balance this with all the equally 'unwise' shots he went for throughout his career and got.

Very often while watching White I would find myself on the edge of my seat shouting at the television: "Don't go for it, Jimmy" and then when it went in, wiping the sweat from my brow and gasping, "Nice one, my son."

When Jimmy hit that green, I thought of the comment convicted murderer Gary Gilmore uttered just prior to his execution: "Let's do it." He was refusing to play around any more. It was kill or be killed. Similarly the Ginger Magician licked his cat-like lips and pounced.

Though it was ultimately a futile gesture in a losing cause, people liked to see Jimmy taking on shots such as that green, even if he missed it by a mile. It was the spirit of adventure that Dennis Taylor would employ with success on the last black against Davis in their famous final the following year. Jimmy had frailty, vulnerability. You suffered for and with him. His soulful face said everything. The first dream died with that green. Davis was always lurking, like Reardon had been with Higgins years earlier. Reardon was a former policeman. Davis was the son of a Primary school teacher and looked like a teacher himself. He was spanking Jimmy. But audience loyalty lay with the pupil.

Davis lifted the trophy over his head to the booing of large sections of the audience. He was the first man to retain the title at the Crucible and he relished the experience. "I knew Jimmy would come back at me," he said in the post-match interview, but what good was the recovery when it didn't translate into victory? It was the first of many such occurences in Jimmy's career.

Why could he not find the extra gear at the death? I couldn't put my finger on it. When he was trailing by a large margin he seemed to relax, but then when he got close to victory Jimmy's nerves came back. In this he was different from Higgins. You felt if Higgins came back to 17-16 he would have put Davis under the cosh. But this was all academic now. The white knight hadn't come over the hill on his charger. The miracle didn't occur, so the bubbly would have to be put on ice.

In the year of 1984 Big Brother once again was world champion. George Orwell would have turned in his grave.

Maybe, I thought, looking at this disgruntled young man, maybe a little part of Jimmy White has to die every now and then so that he can carry home the laurels. Maybe a little part of his natural ebullience has to pass away so that a new, implacable entity may be born out of the ashes. But he must stop riding into the valley of death at a canter, must eliminate that rush of blood to the head that has cost him so much in so short a span of time.

A passage from Ernest Hemingway's *A Farewell to Arms* sprang to mind:

'If people bring so much courage to this world, the world has to kill them to break them, so of course it kills them. The world breaks everyone and afterwards many are strong at the broken places. But those that will not break it kills. It kills the very good and the very gentle and the very brave impartially. If you are none of those you can be sure it will kill you too, but there will be no special hurry.'

Jimmy was the moral victor of that 1984 final, even if he was the actual loser. As the saying went, 'You never beat Jimmy White, you just score more points than him.' But what good was tea and sympathy to the 22-year-old?

Harvey Lisberg went into some detail about 'the Jimmy problem', saying, "Everybody that surrounds him is bad news. They're all drinking, they're smoking marijuana, whatever. They're on women – three women, five women, men – there's no limit in snooker. There's nothing normal about it. And this kid is there in the middle of it all." He even talked about putting Jimmy on a drinking ban during the season. Lisberg declared that he didn't mind if Jimmy got absolutely paralytic from May to September, but during the snooker season he wanted him dry.

After the match, Alex Higgins looked to be more on the point of tears than Jimmy. There was nobody the Hurricane liked to see winning matches more than Jimmy, and nobody he loved seeing lose more than Davis, a man the Irishman had once said was "about as exciting as watching your stools float." Davis resisted responding to such insults, refusing to be drawn into the fray. He knew his record against Higgins was exemplary, so to engage in a bout of verbal interplay would have been counter-productive. He admitted Alex was a much more exciting player to watch than himself, but maintained he wasn't as quick as he looked.

"He's fast in his movements between shots," Davis allowed, "not during the break-building itself." Davis also said Higgins had a terrific instinct for survival, which was another way of saying he had a great safety game. "But at the end of the day, Alex just doesn't get enough balls in the holes."

Higgins was so protective of Jimmy at this time that a few days before the final, when he overheard the journalist John Hennessy telling Kirk Stevens that he believed Stevens would have given Davis a harder match than Jimmy, he reared up at him and angrily told him to leave the kid alone. It was almost as if Higgins had adopted Jimmy like a surrogate son, as if he was trying to protect him from the snooker jungle by putting him in a box that had 'Fragile, Handle With Care' inscribed on it. Jimmy was content to let him do this, accepting the blandishments of the elder statesman, the punch-drunk fighter who'd bounced back from the ropes in 1982 and then taken the young ingenue under his wing. In their forays into Nighttown one imagined it was Higgins who was the pacemaker and Jimmy the one who rode shotgun.

Davis also held a bogey over Jimmy's friend Tony Meo at this time, beating him in the 1984 Lada Classic in a match that went down to the wire. It was a best of 17 and the score stood at 8-8. They were on the colours. Tony looked all set to clear the table when a shout went out from the crowd as he got down to play the yellow. He missed it as a result and Davis took the match. In December of that year Meo led Davis 7-4 in the Coral UK quarter-finals at Preston, but lost the match 9-8. The following year he led Davis 8-7 in the semi-final of the English Professional Championship, but lost 9-8. Berated afterwards by an interviewer for not going for his shots, Meo lamented, "What shots?" Like Jimmy, he knew that The Nugget ground you down so much that it was difficult to get into a rhythm. As a result of that, slowly but surely you felt yourself being drawn into his slower style of play. The resultant tactical frames infinitely suited the Romford man more.

Barry Hearn often joked about Tony, as he did about Jimmy, usually unkindly. After Meo joined the Matchroom team he opined, "If only I could persuade him not to concede before the referee has tossed the coin he'd be all right." Asked once if he'd insured Meo's hands he replied, "No, I've insured his brain. It's a much smaller premium."

Parts of Jimmy's 1984/5 season were impressive even if he didn't fully deliver on the promise of the world final with Davis. He won the Carlsberg Challenge and reached the final of the Langs Scottish Masters. Davis beat him there, and also in the quarter-final of the Coral UK Open. But then came the usual downer as he went out in round two of the Mercantile Credit Classic to a player ranked many places below him, the Australian Warren King. Cliff Thorburn knocked him out of the Benson & Hedges Masters in the semi-final, Silvino Francisco beat him in round one of the Dulux British Open before going on to win the title in a controversial final against Kirk Stevens.

Then came the resurgence. Jimmy won the Irish Masters, defeating Alex Higgins 9-5 in the final, and it looked like a good omen for him in the world championships. He beat Wayne Jones in the first round at Sheffield and then Tony Meo 13-11 in the next. In the third round he found Tony Knowles a sterner challenge. He took the first frame but in the second he knocked in a black by accident when potting a red and Knowles pounced. After that frame Jimmy was always behind. Neither did he look comfortable, even in frames where Knowles needed snookers. He didn't seem to have a match strategy, mixing the slam-bang style and some uncharacteristic conservatism. Knowles played a solid game, waiting for his chances and then scoring significantly. Jimmy was typically magical in patches, but he looked tense throughout the encounter. He never really hit top form. When he missed he often seemed to leave the table like an orchard, with the reds scattered across it waiting to be picked. Knowles, a steady but unexceptional player, was only too happy to oblige. Final score: 13-9 to the Bolton man.

1985 had the most talked-about final of the modern game with over 18 million people tuning in to watch the unfancied Dennis Taylor finally knock Steve Davis off his pedastal with the last ball of the last frame. It's a match people still talk about, largely because Taylor, like the Jimmy of a year before, came back from a huge deficit (he was 8-0 down at one point). Before the final Davis was 1/3 to win, with Taylor at 9/4. After Davis went 8-0 up, the odds on an 18-0 whitewash dropped from 300/1 to 100/1. But after Taylor put a frame on the board the whole complexion of the match changed. With his 'no surrender' attitude, Taylor's Joe 90 glasses almost misted over with glee. Suddenly, there was everything to play for.

As the 11th frame got underway a TV camera squeaked and Taylor went over to it and pretended to pour oil into it with his cue. With this simple gesture he was letting Davis know the pressure wasn't getting to him. If only Jimmy could have had that kind of composure in his tussles with Davis. Sometimes it's not only about the shots you play, but the attitude you bring to the table. Taylor always saw himself as someone who brought a smile back into snooker. Jimmy, on the contrary, was inscrutable.

Taylor fought his way back to just 9-7 down at the end of the first day's play. Davis had gone from a near-impregnable position to realising he was now in a match. You didn't have to be a genius to know which of the two men went to bed the happier.

The following day Davis re-asserted himself, going ahead again, but he was still unable to shake off the dogged Irishman. He went 17-15 up, needing just one more frame to win, but once again Taylor clawed his way back into contention. Against all the odds Taylor forced the match to a deciding frame. This seemed to go on for an eternity. We were in the wee hours of the morning and the match would be decided by the last four colours, all of which Taylor needed. He potted brown, blue and then pink. The World Championship was down to one ball.

Taylor attempted a cheeky double on the black and missed. Davis was less adventurous, keeping things tight. Taylor finally tried it into the green pocket from distance and missed by a mile. He left a thin cut to the top pocket. Davis got ready to hit it. This was his moment. A shot he would have got seven times out of ten, in his own words.

This was one of the three times. He over-cut it, leaving it close to the top pocket. Surely Taylor couldn't miss this. But in the circumstances, with the World title resting on this one shot, anything could be missed.

Taylor potted it and went wild, shaking his cue above his head like a spear, stamping it into the ground. He smiled and wagged his finger. David Vine came out for the interviews. Davis looked as if he no longer believed in God. Vine asked him what happened with his last shot. "You saw it in black and white," said Davis. Tragedy had driven him to make the best pun of his life.

At 22 minutes after midnight on 29 April 1985, Dennis Taylor wrote himself into snooker legend. As he put it himself, "I became an overnight success after 13 years." The shot on the black netted him £25,000 alone (i.e. the difference between winning and losing the match). In Coalisland he became a superstar, like his friend Barry McGuigan the boxer. Taylor's fans wanted the Popemobile to bring him back to Ireland. They said his cue was made in Lourdes. The religion of snooker had begun.

This was all very exciting, to be sure, but the snooker wasn't of the same quality as it had been in the White-Davis final of the previous year. Should this matter? Of course it should, but as commentators often point out, some games are more intriguing when players are missing pots and making mistakes. Especially when so many games are won with large breaks today, cat-and-mouse exchanges get audiences on the edges of their seats. After Davis winning in 1983 and 1984, it was a breath of fresh air to see a dogged old warhorse like Taylor wrest the title from him.

Jimmy and Taylor had some good battles over the years. One of their matches had an interesting backstory. It concerns a lady called Bridget Gervin from Coalisland in Northern Ireland whom the RUC had to forcibly remove from her house one night, minutes before a 1,000lb bomb demolished it. The reason for her stubbornness was that she wanted to see the end of a match between Jimmy and Taylor. She owned the club where Taylor used to play, so he was her priority, but I doubt if she'd have stood up to the RUC if Taylor had been playing someone like Davis – except in that 1985 world final.

Could Jimmy have beaten Davis in the 1984 final if he'd scrapped like Taylor? I think so. This was always going to be Taylor's only world title – a one off. Higgins put it crudely ("Every dog has his day"), but we all knew it was a match won more by perspiration than inspiration.

Having said that, Davis won more matches with Jimmy than he had a right to. Sometimes I felt this was more due to psychology than anything else.

Jimmy once said to me, "Players used to check out of their hotel rooms when they found they were up against Davis in the draw." Okay, he was good, but was he that good? A lot of it was to do with the way he carried himself, and his attitude to the game. To me he always seemed to begin matches with an invisible lead. When he came to the table he didn't seem to need to be warmed up. Most players played a few nervous shots at the beginnings of matches, but Davis seemed to come to the table as if he'd just been practising for five hours. (In fact he probably had.) He always viewed the first frame as crucial. If he won it his opponent had to win two to go ahead. He liked to stamp his supremacy early, whip frames off before the other guy hardly realised the match was on. Not necessarily through brilliance, but rather application.

The Irish broadcaster Gay Byrne had Jimmy on his late night talk show once and he asked him, "Do you ever pray before a match?" Jimmy thought for a moment before replying, "Only when I'm playing Steve Davis."

Jimmy's contract with Harvey Lisberg ran out in 1985. Both men felt they were wrong for each other, so there was no question of renewing it. He then spent a short time with Howard Kruger, a jetsetting manager from a company called Framework which had set itself up against Barry Hearn's Matchroom stable. But Kruger lacked Hearn's nous. Hearn, a chartered accountant and self-made man, had bought a chain of run-down snooker halls in 1975 and went on to form the Matchroom syndicate, his fame and fortune largely attributable to taking Davis under his wing early on in the Romford prodigy's career. The pair went on to become strong friends.

Snooker was enjoying a huge surge in popularity at this time. When Matchroom (which comprised players like Meo, Griffiths, Thorne, Taylor and Foulds as well as Davis) brought out the song 'Snooker Loopy', written by cockney popsters Chas and Dave, it went to Number 6 in the charts, an incredible feat considering the fact that the song was never going to rank in the realm of pop classics.

Framework tried to emulate that success with a song called 'The Wanderer' which had Knowles, Jimmy, Alex and Kirk Stevens. Stevens was only on it because he'd called to the recording studio that day to give Higgins a lift to London. Maybe that said everything about Framework's sense of planning – or lack of it. The backing group was called 'Four Away', which again was significant. The song didn't make the Top 50.

Perhaps inevitably, Jimmy left Framework for the Hearn stable, which didn't impress Lisberg. "No way is he going to be a good product for a sponsor to take on," he moaned. "He isn't going to start selling Horlicks." Hearn perhaps feared this, and signed Jimmy up with some reluctance. He was never a fan of Jimmy's temperament, feeling his association with people like Higgins (whom Hearn wouldn't touch with a barge pole) defined him. He also felt he under-performed in tournaments considering his immense natural ability.

The fact that Jimmy was now being handled by the man who also looked after his old adversary was a supreme irony. It was almost like the Beatles and the Rolling Stones having the same manager. How long would it take before the pressure cooker exploded?

It's no accident that Hearn subsequently went into boxing management. If Davis treated snooker like a chess game, Hearn saw it as unadulterated pugilism where only one man was left standing at the end. Alex Higgins might have been more physically aggressive than Hearn or Davis, but these two men were equally ruthless in a more subtle fashion.

It seemed his new manager didn't actually rate Jimmy that highly either. When people said Jimmy was the most natural player in the game, Hearn quipped, "Being natural means you miss." Winning meant everything to this man, as did money. (The joke went that the 'H' in his name was silent.) Hearn didn't look forward to the task of keeping Jimmy under wraps, which was somewhat akin to holding a tiger by the tail. He vaguely subscribed to the generally held theory that Jimmy was unmanageable. "If I ever get a heart attack," Hearn once told him, "it will be because of you." Hearn's business-oriented manner was infinitely more suited to somebody like Davis, whom you could set your watch by.

"The sadness," Hearn said once, "is that we need the Higginses and the Whites, these flamboyant natural players. We need them to keep the game fresh and alive and exciting, but from a commercial point of view nobody needs them at all. It would be a disaster to have them front any campaign. No multi-national would touch them, which means they can only ever get their incomes from tournaments and live-show exhibitions, which is a dwindling market."

This summation betrays a profound ignorance of anything that conduces to cult appeal. Not everyone can be (or would want to be) sanitised. Entertainment needs its Sid Vicious as much, if not more than its Cliff Richard. The Jimmy that pulled in the crowds was the same Jimmy that sometimes failed to turn up. You couldn't have one without the other.

Hearn also said, "Jimmy has a flair for living. When he was 12-years-old he was as worldly as a 40-year-old and as naive as a 4-year-old . He would work out a Yankee, but couldn't name the capital of France."

Jimmy's reply? "That's easy. It's Monte Carlo."

VODKA, LAGER AND BENSONS

JIMMY'S 1985/6 SEASON began with a bang. He went to Australia to compete in the Winfield Masters, but found himself jet-lagged after the 20-hour flight. Solution? A game of snooker. Who was waiting for him in the local hall, but big Bill Werbeniuk, the Canadian who famously drank six pints of lager before each match to 'steady his hands'. Werbeniuk had been in Australia a few days already. He challenged Jimmy to an unofficial money match, feeling confident that he'd take the jet-lagged Englishman. Jimmy, as John Parrott wrote in his autobiography, 'looked as if he'd just rolled out of a hedge backwards', but he couldn't resist the bet. They decided to play for a pound a point. Ten minutes later Jimmy had knocked in a maximum and the Canadian was 147 nicker down. In the next frame Jimmy made a 106. At which point Werbeniuk decided to call it a day.

Typically, Jimmy didn't win the Australian event, being beaten by Tony Meo (the eventual winner) in the semi-final, but he won the next tournament on the calendar, the Carlsberg Challenge, defeating Parrott in the semi-final and Higgins in the final. Then came two crazy marathon matches with Cliff Thorburn. Jimmy lost the one he should have won and won the one he should have lost. So what else was new?

The first came in the Goya Matchroom tournament, in which Jimmy impressively beat Warren King in the first round, Dean Reynolds even more easily 5-1 in the next, and then Davis in the quarter-final, before taking out Neal Foulds 9-5 in the semis. That left Jimmy facing Cliff Thorburn in the final. Amusingly, he led 7-1 after the first session. Paul Hatherell, the tournament director, expected the match to be over with a session to spare and wondered if he could arrange an exhibition to fill in the rest of the night. But things didn't quite work out like that.

Thorburn described Jimmy's first seven frames as "the finest exhibition of snooker I've ever seen." But Jimmy still had six more to win, so Thorburn decided to slow him down a bit. Critics of Thorburn might say he spent the lion's share of his career 'slowing players down a bit'.

Jimmy went 74 up in the 8th frame. There were only four reds left, so Thorburn needed four snookers. Jimmy then potted one of the four reds, but in doing so jumped the cue ball off the table. Now the score was 74-4. Even allowing for the foul, Thorburn now needed five snookers. Most players wouldn't even have come back to the table. Thorburn did, mainly to get his cue arm going, it being the first frame of the night session. But then he started to lay some good snookers and Jimmy started to foul. He left free balls in trying to get out of two of them, an unforgiveable sin when one is leading by so much. Thorburn freakishly won the frame, which disturbed Jimmy's mindset hugely. Brian Clough used to say it only takes a second to score a goal in soccer. Likewise, it only takes a second to change the course of a snooker game. That second came when Jimmy jumped the cue ball off the table. Winning a virtually unwinnable frame like that was worth six to Thorburn because it changed the whole complexion of the match. The psychological advantage was with him. One was reminded of Clive Everton's comment, "Scar tissue forms on boxers' eyebrows but in snooker players' minds."

Of this particular match Everton said, "White's feeling of omnipotence was shaken." Jimmy started to feel he could lose this match and Thorburn started to feel he could win. Not might, but could.

Thorburn must have been thinking, *if I can win a frame from needing five snookers, I can win a match from 7-1 behind*. He certainly started to play that way. Even a glimmer of hope is enough to steady a player on the shot and conversely eat into his opponent's mind. Thorburn continued to stick daggers into Jimmy and went to bed that night trailing only 8-6. In a way he felt like he was leading.

Hatherell, needless to say, was chuffed that Thorburn instigated the about-turn. Attendances hadn't been great during the week (one afternoon had attracted the grand sum of 28 customers), but now that the stage was set for a dramatic finale they were streaming in. Tony Meo, sitting at the back of the auditorium, could hardly bear to watch. Thorburn's mindset was similar to Davis's. He was capable of making snooker look like pulling teeth. If he had to bring in a tent and camp beside the table overnight to beat Jimmy, so be it. Let's not forget he once finished a match against Terry Griffiths in the second round of the 1983 World Championships at 3.51 a.m. He could bore Jimmy to death.

And so he did. Thorburn triumphed by 12 frames to 10, Jimmy's spirit having been crushed by the comeback. It was like death by a thousand cuts. Remember, we're talking about a player who once said, "I always feel I'm on for a 10-9 win when I'm 0-9 down." That sort of attitude made Jimmy a crowd favourite but he couldn't keep up his rhythm or momentum to blast Thorburn off the table.

Thorburn said of Jimmy, "If you lose your concentration with him you're gone because there's no time to recover. You can be in control of the play for 90 per cent of the time and lose on just one shot." He added, "I get more sense of achievement out of beating him than I do with most players because he's so difficult to keep at bay. On top of that he's such a pleasure to play because he's such a gentleman. There's never any aggro. Win or lose, nothing fazes him."

This isn't strictly true. Thorburn was probably thinking about the contrast between Jimmy and Higgins (whom Thorburn has rattled sabres with more than once) when he made that comment, but Jimmy can be very fazed after a defeat, albeit inwardly.

The clash of styles continued at the Mercantile Credit Classic. Jimmy disposed of another Canadian, Marcel Gavreau, by 5 frames to 2 in the first round and Davis by the same margin in the second. The turning point of this match came in frame six. Davis was leading by 3 frames to 2 and by 58 points to 2, but then, strangely for him, he missed a straightforward red and Jimmy cleared the table to square the match. After that Jimmy's confidence grew and he reeled off the next three frames in record time. His semi-final against a stolid Rex Williams (whom he expected to trounce) was much closer. Jimmy squeezed him out eventually by 9 frames to 7.

That brought Jimmy up against Thorburn again in the final. As in the Goya he started well, going 4-0 up before the Canadian got into groove and fought back to 4-3 at the end of the session. Jimmy got stuck in a traffic jam before the start of the evening session and was docked a frame, so the score was now level. Thorburn took the next two to leave Jimmy scratching his head in disbelief. "One minute I'm in front," he reminisced later, "and the next I'm right out of it. I didn't rightly know what was happening." Thorburn went 8-5 up, but Jimmy pulled him back to 8-7 at the end of the session to leave himself in contention.

At 9-9 Jimmy found a second wind and capitalised on a poor safety shot by Thorburn to seize the initiative again. In the 20th frame he made a sparkling 117 clearance to forge further ahead. In the next he built up a 54 point lead only to see Thorburn steal the frame on the black. Would his confidence waver as it had in their previous battle? It looked that way when he lost the 22nd frame, so now it was honours even. Soon it was 12-12 with one frame to play: time to get out the valium.

I was watching this match on television at home with my aforementioned brother Hugo, who started to annoy me with his comments about what was going on. In a temper I slammed the door shut and went down to the pub to watch the climax of the match, shaking so much I could hardly breathe as I stormed down the road.

Thorburn racked up 49 points in the final frame before Jimmy got off the mark. When all the reds were potted Jimmy was still significantly behind. He needed all six colours to notch up the first ranking tournament win of his career, but he missed the yellow. Thorburn potted it and then fluked the green to leave Jimmy needing a snooker. After Jimmy potted the brown and blue he was now 17 points adrift, with a greatly reduced chance of securing a snooker as only pink and black remained on the table.

I always felt that winning frames like this bored Jimmy. In fact I once saw him conceding a frame in Goffs when he could still win and there were five reds on the table. But then, from nowhere, he produced what I can only describe as a stroke of genius; a dynamic snooker on the pink. The shot will linger forever in my mind. It was a snooker Thorburn failed to negotiate. Jimmy stepped in to pot a great pink and black for victory. He never cut it closer than this: winning a major on the last ball of the last frame.

When I got back to the house Hugo thought I was going to be over the moon, but for some reason I couldn't celebrate. All the tension had taken its toll. I was just numb, despite the fact that it was the first time anyone had won a tournament in a final frame after needing a snooker since Ray Reardon beat John Spencer 4-3 in the Park Drive 2000 event in 1971.

Jimmy celebrated his phenomenal victory in the Credit Classic by getting legless and by adopting a puppy he called, perhaps inevitably, 'Mercantile'. He won the match by digging down into some subliminal part of himself. It was an escape Houdini would have envied. This was the flipside of his unpredictability, the ability to get so fed up of his laxities that he alchemised himself into the kind of player even an on-form Davis would fear. When he was buzzing, we all knew, he could reel off half a dozen frames on the spin without his opponent having played a bad shot.

Thorburn's ambition was never to let Jimmy out of the paddock. It was a similar type of blueprint (or rather greenprint) employed by Jack Charlton when he managed the Irish soccer team. Winning became not so much a question of playing well as making your opponent play badly. It may not have been pretty, but by Christ, it was effective. The Irish soccer team got into the last eight of the World Cup under Charlton, which wasn't bad for a small country, even if the players are only Irish by qualification. (They all live in England and some were born outside of the Emerald Isle.) They did this not by showing class, but graft. It's something Thorburn, the archetypal grinder, knew plenty about.

Jimmy met Thorburn in a third final that season, the Canadian winning 9-5 in the final of the Benson & Hedges Masters. His gameplan was the same as it had always been against Jimmy: containment. This time it worked. "If I attempted to outpot Jimmy it would have been a joke," Thorburn admitted after the match.

Thorburn of course is gone from the game now, having been 'found out' by the younger players who have no interest in tapdancing around with safety shots for three hours. These people, blooded in the Jimmy White school of winning or losing fast, make a point of splitting the pack early and going for broke. Thorburn hasn't been able to live with this, nor with the fact that the overall standard of potting has taken a quantum leap.

Jimmy says he partied for a week after snatching the Mercantile from the fire. By now he was threatening to dethrone Higgins as the People's Champion. His flair, his punchy style, the fact that he declared fouls on himself, all this and more endeared him to the British public, not all of whom were snooker lovers. He was a crowdpleaser and a crowdpuller. He had everything Higgins had and more. Maybe he was the new face of snooker, a delicate-faced lad that women wanted to mother, if not bed.

Jimmy was certainly turning heads within the media, who'd latched on to the Whirlwind as the next big thing and loved his refreshing approach to the game. After he was beaten by Thorburn in the Goya, *The Times's* correspondent wrote of Jimmy, 'He makes snooker seem a gay, chivalrous thing, one in which a young man could happily toss his life away with a smile. If Harry Hotspur had been a snooker player, he would have been like Jimmy White of Tooting.'

This was how Gordon Burn described him: 'The tasty gear, the delinquent shuffle and the wide-boy lingo, the cigarette clamped between thumb and first finger and cupped behind the back, all this signals a rough-and-ready upbringing as part of a large family on a tougher-than-tough council estate.' More worryingly, for his minders, he added, 'Basically Jimmy has the standard bad boy build of 9 stone of concave sinew and gristle, kept that way by a regular daily intake of vodka, lager and Bensons.'

The journalist Sue Mott declared her mother always worried about Jimmy: 'One glance at that whey-faced waif hunched tensely over his snooker cue, a pallid testimony to the ravages of beer and biryani, was enough to confirm her worst suspicions – he wasn't looking after himself properly. She longed to administer steak and kidney pies.'

My own mother felt the same way. Maybe all of our mothers did. It was the little-boy-lost look that first entranced Maureen.

Jimmy had big hopes of defending his Goya trophy in 1986, but had what we might call a 'Jimmy moment' in going under to Ken Owens (Ken who?) in the third round. Owens was playing in his first professional tournament. Another example of the White quandary.

Jimmy held on to his Benson & Hedges Irish Masters title in 1986, beating Willie Thorne 9-5 in a high quality final. He'd beaten Higgins by the same scoreline in the 1985 final. The came the World Championships. At Sheffield he faced Davis and everyone expected a thrilling encounter, but Jimmy was destroyed 13-5. Far from the knife-edge drama anyone who saw their 1984 final might have expected, Jimmy, to quote Gordon Burn, was 'left looking like somebody waiting at a country busstop.'

It was good for snooker that Davis was again beaten in the world final that year, especially when it was by no-hoper Joe Johnson, a player who once claimed he couldn't win a match on television. He surely picked a good place to start, handing Davis a fair old hammering of 18-12 in an exhibition of near-faultless snooker.

To me that match simply reinforced what Jimmy was missing out on. He could win. If only he could focus for long enough.

In October 1986 Jimmy copperfastened his reputation in the game by lifting the Rothman's Grand Prix trophy. The secret to his success was a close quarter-final victory over a callow Stephen Hendry. Their match went down to the wire, Hendry missing a cut on the blue in the final frame to let Jimmy in. He saw off Silvino Francisco in the semi-finals and in the final, incredibly, faced Rex Williams, playing as if his life depended on it. Williams had thrashed both Higgins and Davis 5-1 before a marathon semi-final against Neal Foulds which he scraped through 9-8.

Against Jimmy, Williams knew his safety would be the key, but he potted a few balls too in what he surely knew must be his last hurrah. It wasn't to be. Jimmy got the measure of the 54-year-old from 2-5 down and rattled off eight of the next nine frames to take the title. Now, at least, Jimmy was becoming a regular winner. His talent was beginning to be fulfilled.

* * *

The fortunes of the Hurricane, in contrast, began to wane. Following an incident in which he head-butted tournament director Paul Hatherall during the UK Championship after being asked to submit a urine sample for drug testing, Higgins's wild ways continued. After a row with his girlfriend Siobhan Kidd he broke his foot while indulging in some freefall parachuting (without a parachute) from a window ledge in her house. Bloodied but unbowed, 'Hopalong' Higgins went on to win the Benson & Hedges Masters Final 9-8 against Stephen Hendry in what was to be his last ranking victory.

Jimmy continued to socialise with Alex but in his heart of hearts he must have felt that his old buddy and sometime idol was losing the plot. Maureen threw Higgins out of their house one night when he was acting the maggot, feeling no hint of sympathy for him as he stumbled down the road. The next morning he was as chipper as ever on the phone, saying, "Hello, babes, is James available please?" All Maureen could do was shake her head.

"He can drive you to distraction one minute," she said, "and have you in stitches the next." Jimmy added, "He's a nightmare to be with unless he's winning."

Normal service – for Jimmy White at least – was resumed when he was beaten in the fourth round of the British Open in 1987 by John Spencer, losing one of the frames after Spencer needed five snookers. Barry Hearn, his unforgiving manager, chastised Jimmy severely over this defeat, feeling Spencer was way past his best. This sort of thing happened way too often with Jimmy and a lot of it was due to poor match preparation or over-confidence. It was something he desperately needed to address, but usually didn't due to his carefree ways. It led Hearn to despair of him ever reaching the top of the snooker tree.

1987 was to further define Jimmy's rivalry with Davis. In the Tennents UK Open final he gave The Nugget a real fright, but eventually succumbed 14-16. If that was close, the Mercantile Credit Classic final was even closer. Jimmy hadn't beaten Davis in a final for six years, but he started well, leading 2-0 before Davis got going. There was nothing between them as the final developed; 5-5, 7-7, 11-11. Davis made a 47 in the 23rd frame to go 1 up with 2 to play. Jimmy levelled and went 35-0 up in the decider, but made a fatal error in splitting the pack after missing a long red. Davis, who would never have let the cue ball stray anywhere near the sacred pack with a lead like that, replied with a 35. He then played a killer snooker on Jimmy, nestling the cue ball in behind the yellow at the bottom end of the table with the reds spread invitingly around the black. Jimmy failed to get out of it and Davis did what Davis was always good at doing – closing a match out with a steady combination of potting and strategy. It was the old story once again, Jimmy promising so much but failing to second guess his old rival at the death. Result: 13-12 to The Nugget.

Impetuosity had struck again.

But then, as if dismissing the agony of such a defeat without a thought or care, in the Dulux British Open two months later, Jimmy romped to the title, proving too strong for Mike Hallett, Rex Williams, John Spencer, Cliff Thorburn and, in the final, Neal Foulds. The fact that Davis went out early – he was sensationally beaten by John Virgo in the quarter finals – must have boosted Jimmy's confidence.

He was second favourite for the World Championship that year, but he knew he'd have to dispose of Davis at some stage if he was to realise that dream. He met him in the semi-final after brushing Dene O'Kane aside 13-6 in the quarters. Davis proved a sterner test, leading 9-6 after the first day's play. The match really hinged on the next frame, in which Jimmy led by 73 points. He thought it was in the bag, but Davis had different ideas and slowly but surely ate away at Jimmy's lead, aided and abetted by a fluky black and some clever snookers. Losing that frame hurt. Badly. "It knocked him bandy for three frames after that," was Jimmy's father's estimation of things.

The rest was a foregone conclusion. Davis went into cruise control to win by 16 frames to 11. Jimmy had yet to beat Davis at the Crucible after three tries. Davis went on to win the world title again that year, annoyed with himself that he'd let both 1985 and 1986 slip by. His opponent in the final was Joe Johnson, his shock conqueror the year before, surely a man Jimmy would have swamped in a hail of potting.

But while he was proving his worth on the table, it was outside the competitive arena that Jimmy was really hitting the headlines. The *Sunday People* ran a story that year entitled 'Jimmy's Secret Shame', which alleged that he was hooked on cocaine. Later that year a blonde called Kim Drewer told the same paper that she'd slept with him after being given drugs at a party. Jimmy maintained these stories were "all complete bollocks", although he admitted he'd smoked a joint or two in his time. But snooker players got tested all the time "so we can't afford to go snorting drugs all day". On the other hand, "When shit like that is thrown at you, it tends to stick. That's the frustrating thing. I thought about suing them, but it's more trouble than it's worth," he said.

He continued to show what he was worth on the green baize by beating Neal Foulds in the final of the Dulux British Open to bag the third ranking title of his career. It was made even more special by dint of the fact that he came back from 4-0 down. The match turned on the 15th frame. Foulds was 8-6 up at that point, but when Jimmy closed to one instead of three overnight the head of steam was with him. As it happened, Foulds would only win one more frame and he admitted afterwards: "If you aren't playing well, and I wasn't, he tends to give you an inferiority complex. To compare Jimmy with Steve [Davis], I would say that Steve is harder to play against, but he can't demoralise you like Jimmy can."

I felt Jimmy had a lot of interesting stories to tell about his life, so I tried to interview him again that year, this time going through the official channels of Benson & Hedges, the people behind the Irish Masters. The idea was good, but Kevin Norton, the tournament organiser, said to me, "Jimmy is too hot at the moment. You're one of about 20 journalists who've approached me for an interview." In fact I wasn't even a full-time journalist then, nor in the union. I was just freelancing after school, a 'fan with a typewriter' to use an expression in vogue then.

Frustrated, I had to content myself with watching his matches at the Masters from the gods when I had the money to go out to Kildare or on the television when I hadn't. I was in a teaching job now, so had enough time to drive down to the venue for the evening sessions as the school I was working in closed each day at 2.30. I was also playing a bit of snooker myself. Like Jimmy I'd become hooked on the game from my pre-teens, but unlike Jimmy I had no natural ability. Having said that, I was on the team that won the League for North Dublin one year, although I'll admit that hardly compares. I looked at the trophy every now and then when my playing was useless (which was most of the time) to remind myself of the glory days.

I rang London often to try and set something up with Jimmy over there. Being a teacher, I had two months free in the summer and thought we might be able to get something going during the holidays, when the snooker season was also in recess. I knew he was in big demand for exhibitions and the like, but surely there was some window they could squeeze me into.

It was possible, but not likely, his very friendly secretaries told me time and again on my increasingly desperate phone calls. Sometimes I even called from public boxes. I remember on one occasion getting through to the office of Jimmy's manager. Kirk Stevens picked up the phone and heard a cascade of coins going into it at my end. "You better get out of that box, my friend," he said, "it sounds like they're taking all your money away."

Every time I tried to set something up it seemed as if there was an invisible Fort Knox around Jimmy. But then, finally, I managed it. An agreement. Jimmy was to be over playing an exhibition at Goffs and he would see me. I was high as a kite with glee.

We set up the interview for noon on a day when he was playing a few hours later. I arrived at Goffs in plenty of time and searched high and low for Jimmy, but nobody knew where he was. I eventually tracked him down to Alex Higgins's room, where I found him playing cards with some other fellers. When I discovered him and told him who I was and what I wanted he said he had to get some practice in and could I arrange our interview for some other time. "Sure," I said, but inside myself I was thinking, *Screw you, Jimmy.*

I suggested that we play a frame or two together anywhere of his choice. He said I'd have to organise it through his manager, so we were back to square one. And so it went on. It was another hard luck story for me.

Every time he came to Ireland to play in the Irish Masters I used to ring him at the hotel he stayed in. Each time, to my surprise, I was put through to his room immediately. When I said "Good luck" he invariably replied, "Cheers, mate, I'll try my best." Jimmy rarely had anything more to add, not being the most loquacious, but he was invariably gentlemanly. I was always a bit nervous making these calls, but I continued to make them, driven as I was to have some quality time with my hero.

Just occasionally I was brave enough to add some advice onto the end of my call; comments like, "Don't give anything away for nothing. Everyone knows you take on one too many balls in a frame. Don't make it easy for them."

I also told him not all frames had to end in seven minutes, and not all of them with Jimmy White centuries. Like a donkey that keeps wandering off the main path, I felt he needed someone to hit him over the head with a hard stick to get the best out of himself. "You don't have to go for glory every time," I told him, "your fans will tolerate morsels of stodginess if it means victory."

On another phone call I said, "Higgins claims he'd kill to win the world title. Maybe the first thing you have to do is kill the part of yourself that loves the game and make it into work." For Jimmy that would have been too much of a compromise, but I thought it was the only way to go.

Did he pay attention? He'd often say "Okay, mate" or something like that, but I doubted he ever really listened to these comments. Why should he? Who was I to tell Jimmy White what to do. If I knew how to play the game, why wasn't I out there in the heat of battle rather than watching it from the comfort of my sofa in Dublin 5? But I knew that even if I was his coach, or a fellow pro, the chances are that any advice proferred would go in one ear and probably not even make it to the other.

This bothered me. I firmly believed that if Jimmy could straighten out a few small things in his game he'd start to win more. I felt he was losing matches because he was in denial about these faults. He promised he'd change, but I grew to take everything he said with a pinch of salt. In the next tournament he'd get a kick, or the white would go in-off, or he'd get a tickle on a red he didn't want which would knock him out of position and he'd play a reckless shot to play himself back in.

It was always the way it had been and always the way it would continue to be.

Jimmy White the gallant loser, the romantic vagabond, his own worst enemy, potting reds as if they were going out of fashion and then in one insane moment throwing away what had taken years to build up.

I made dozens of calls to him during the 1987 Irish Masters, and he even arranged to meet me a couple of times, but – perhaps inevitably – he let me down. On the final day of the event I rang again and this time the porter told me he'd checked out of his room. I decided to try him one last time and amazingly Jimmy answered the phone. I had been told another lie to add to the pattern of the past five days, a pattern that made me wonder at times if it wasn't the Pope I was trying to meet. Jimmy apologised profusely for missing me so many times. "My life is quite chaotic at the moment," he said, his voice tinged with sadness. He'd been going for his hat-trick of Irish Masters titles, but lost the deciding frame of his match with Willie Thorne two days previously.

"I'll meet you tomorrow," he promised, and I laughed. I told him that if I had a penny for every time I'd been told that I'd almost be as rich as he was. "No," he said, "this time I mean it. Most of the other players are gone home now. There'll be no distractions."

The next morning I drove down to Newbridge. When I rang Jimmy's hotel room I half-expected him to have checked out, but he answered the phone and said he'd be down in half an hour. I ordered two pints of Smithwicks from the bar, one for myself to relax me and one for a man whose past had been such that I imagined he would be well inured to the rigours of having a beer for breakfast – perhaps to neutralise the effect of all last night's intake.

And then, without warning, there he was. Jimmy White. In front of me. Looking for me.

He arrived in a tracksuit – hardly what I expected from somebody at the forefront of the extended costume drama that is the snooker cosmos – and I proudly shook the hand that had been insured for so many thousands of pounds. "After all these years!" I said as he casually stretched himself out on the sofa, putting his feet up on the cushions as if he was in his own living room.

"I made a 147 yesterday," he said excitedly as he took a sip of the pint, adding, "I nearly got another one after that but the green done me."

Somehow my professional head took over and I managed to control my excitement and wilful desire to simply jabber about how much I loved him to instead ask a series of cogent questions, beginning with whether he was sick about the Thorne defeat (his father had told me backstage how much the Irish Masters had meant to him.)

"I got a kick just as I was starting a break in the last frame," he said. "If it wasn't for that I think I'd have won. But maybe I didn't deserve it. I left him too many openings."

I asked him if this wasn't a problem with his general game, this practice of creating great chances out of nothing and then missing a sitter for no apparent reason.

"I think too many shots ahead," he said, "that's always been my problem. I try to nudge balls into positions early, to get them off the cushions. Sometimes I take a difficult ball for a positional advantage when there's an easy one available. If I get it I can clear the table, if I don't the other player gets in. Either way things get finished soon. It's the game I learned from Alex Higgins."

How much had he modelled his game on Higgins?

"I never modelled my game on any one player. If you asked me who excited me most as a boy I d have to say Alex, but there's more to it than that, You don't set out to imitate people when you play, you set out to pot balls. Any way you know how. It's like hurdles on a racecourse. You're just trying to get over the line, to win frames. It's no secret I play on instinct like he does, and we both go for the big shots, but there are a lot of differences between us. Alex is much more of a safety player these days than a potter. That hasn't happened to me yet."

I wondered aloud if that might be what was wrong with his game. It was a common attitude that safety was the one thing he needed to improve on. "That's not really true," he said. "I can play good safety when I want to, but it bores me. I think I'm good enough to win matches without concentrating on it too much. I'm also winning tournaments now, so maybe I don't need to change my style."

I asked him about his past, about the days on the road with Dodgy Bob. "Playing snooker for your next meal toughens you," he said. "You don't enjoy losing in that situation." But that was hardly the kind of life the young professionals of today lead. "Things are more organised now. Television has taken over the game. Steve Davis contributed a lot to that. He came into the game when it was becoming a big television sport and he suited that. It's all tournaments and ranking points now." Did that make life easier or harder? He couldn't give a straight answer. It made it both. Living life in front of a television camera wasn't easy for a young man.

What about the technical aspects of his game? I mentioned the fact that I didn't think he was going into the cluster of reds with the same bravado as he used to when he first started, that he didn't seem to be using as much power to swivel the cue ball out of the pack after making the pot. Jimmy admitted he had modified his cavalier approach a bit, saying, "I've lost too many frames from going in-off power shots like that, or potting a colour by mistake. These days I usually pick off the reds one by one instead."

I also asked him about the general way he struck the cue ball, the tinny sound he made as he struck it. "I cue very low on the white ball, but also play a lot of stun and screw shots. I rarely hit the cue ball in the same place twice. Snooker is all about mastering side, it makes the positional side of things that much easier," he told me.

I mentioned an incident a few years earlier where he was playing a red the full length of the table and missed it on the way down. Referee John Williams called a foul, but the white ball came off the end cushion at a weird angle and connected with the red on the way back. Even Williams had to break down laughing. "I keep referees on their toes," he said. "They usually don't know what I'm going to do next. Sometimes I don't know myself."

Did he feel he got a fair deal from referees generally? I mentioned an incident a few years earlier where a match between himself and Davis stood at two frames apiece. He'd just committed a foul and there was a possibility of a free ball. The referee said nothing, but when Davis contested the issue Williams took another look and said, "Free ball". Jimmy stood up from his chair and said, "Is that just because it's Steve Davis that says it, John?" It was the first and last time I'd ever seen him confront a referee. Did he feel he had been hard done by in that match? Jimmy skirted the question.

"I don't go out of my way to make friends with referees or to argue with them. They're there to do a job, that's all there is to it," he said. "If you annoy them they can do you in a later match. I try to stay away from them as much as possible." But the fact remained that Jimmy White seemed to have more fouls declared on him than any other player in the game. I mentioned the number of times I'd seen him stopped in mid-break for having been adjudged to have tipped the white ball with his cue while lining up his shot. "The reason that happens is because I use a delicate cue action," he said. "I don't think referees have it in for me. Sometimes I brush the white with my cue and they don't even see it. I have to tell them."

How did he feel about Higgins – could he be turfed out of the game? "He'd want to take the finger out," he said. "He's got about five good years left in him at the most. You don't last long at the top in snooker."

I mentioned the match between himself and Higgins in 1982, the David and Goliath encounter people still talk about as if it were yesterday. "It was a great match to be in, even though I lost. If I beat Alex that year I would have won the world final. I knew I could have taken Ray Reardon."

"Reardon said he could have taken you," I hazarded. Jimmy laughed. "He says that about everyone."

So how did he feel now about losing the Goya from 7-0 up? "That hardened me," Jimmy admitted. Would he change his tactics from now on? He paused a moment. "Everyone gets less spontaneous as they get older. I think more now before I shoot. I've paid for my hastiness in the past, but I know that's what brings the punters in. It's about getting the balance right. It's not what you miss, but what you leave. Some players have a bash now and again and seem to get away with it. It usually costs me. I don't know why. If I did I wouldn't do it."

Was he disappointed about the fact that Tony Drago had overtaken him as the fastest player in the world? "Good for him. It takes the pressure off me. I've never played fast for the sake of it. It's just my style. If I went slower I'd probably miss."

How often had it happened that he did all the hard work in a frame and then, with one rash shot, threw it all away? "I don't plan it that way, mate," he said, "It's not as if I want to lose."

I knew that. It only seemed that way!

"I've got to go now," he said, shaking my hand and putting his cue away. I wished him well in his next match and showed him some articles I'd written about him. He asked me if he could take them with him to his room to read. I said I would be flattered if he did. Before he left I asked him if he'd ever played billiards considering he was so good at close ball control.

"I won the Boy's Championship at billiards at the time you could only pot five reds in a row," he told me. "I gave it up because it was boring. Some people say I could be the reincarnation of the great Australian billiard player, Walter Lindrum. He died in 1960, not long before I was born."

Did he really believe that was possible? A reincarnation of another legendary player? Jimmy shrugged his shoulders and gave me that toothy grin again. "Who knows?"

Later that week I studied the life of Lindrum as best I could. I learned that he'd been born in Australia into a billiards dynasty, that at the age of three he'd lost the top of his right forefinger in an accident, which caused him to become left-handed. A year later he'd almost been killed when a tree fell on the bedroom in which he was sleeping. At five he also nearly died, having fallen into a river and being swept away by the current until he held on to a tuft of grass on the bank.

Lindrum made his first century break at the age of 12, his zealously ambitious father locking him in the practice room for up to 7 hours a day, and sometimes even more. He used to practise the same shot with just two balls for hours on end. He left school (another White similarity) at 14 and had made a 500 break by then. He was a champion at 15 and 2 years later made his first 1,000 break. He once made a century in 29 seconds, and a 1,000 break in 26 minutes. He visited Britain in 1929 and a year later had made over a hundred breaks of 1,000. In 1932 he made a break of 4137. According to Gordon Burn, the author of *Pocket Money*, he was 'thoroughly unreliable over appointments, money and women.'

Sounds familiar, I thought.

There was one story I uncovered which made me believe Jimmy might have something in his belief. Lindrum was playing Joe Davis one day and left the venue in the middle of a break, going back to his hotel where he lay hungover and slumped over a table. Davis prevailed upon him to return and he made a 100 break.

Another day when the tip of his cue was falling off he refused to have it fixed, preferring to watch the girls go by the window of his hotel. When play resumed he made another century.

When Lindrum played his nursery cannons people couldn't even see his face, so low to the balls, so intense was his concentration. This man was so good he destroyed billiards as a spectacle. Nobody could come near him. Eventually he retired, appearing only for exhibitions. Lindrum seemed to be almost bored by his genius.

Finally Walter Lindrum shared two other things with Jimmy: an OBE and a love of horses.

But was Jimmy his reincarnation? All that matters is that Jimmy himself believes it.

THE BATTLING BURTONS

JIMMY CONTINUED HIS rock star lifestyle as the 80s rolled on. He continued to argue with Maureen and then fall into her arms. They were like The Battling Burtons, Richard and Elizabeth, née Taylor, who married and divorced twice in the Hollywood spotlight. Like those screen legends, Jimmy and Maureen couldn't keep away from each other, but neither could they be with each other for any length of time without fireworks.

Jimmy also spent a lot of time in Ireland, a country he took to his heart. He once told Maureen he was going there for three days and stayed six weeks. Most of that time, coincidentally, he spent in the Gresham Hotel in Dublin. Burton and Taylor had a suite there while Burton was filming *The Spy Who Came in from the Cold*.

Maureen eventually grew impatient with Jimmy's antics, matters reaching a head the time she had to sign papers for a new house they were buying and Jimmy was nowhere to be found. She knew there was a large crew of people who covered for him just as Ted Zanicelli did all those years ago when teachers or siblings would go looking for him to get him to go to school. She eventually followed him over to Ireland and up to his hotel room in the Gresham where, after falling off a stool that had been damaged during a drinking session the previous night, she cottoned on to the fact that he was hiding from her in a wardrobe. She summoned the prodigal husband to her and prevailed upon him to sign the papers. Jimmy, suitably contrite, agreed.

Maybe the irony was that it was Maureen who had Irish blood in her, not Jimmy. Maybe she helped him get in touch with his Irish alter ego. In return, Jimmy encouraged Maureen to look up her ancestry, so there was a kind of poetic justice in it all.

Another time Maureen had to cover up a black eye she received after a set-to with Jimmy (he's not sure exactly how she got it). Broadcaster Eamonn Holmes came calling at her door with a camera crew wondering if things were all right with the pair. Maureen assured him they were, but gave Jimmy an ear-bashing when the TV crew left the area.

Throughout this period, his life seemed to be an endless stream of emotional Polyfilla exercises. Cracks had to be covered, and invariably they were. The marriage might have been rocky, but they didn't want to split up, or at least not publicly.

If they resembled the Burtons, in other ways they were like a prickly brother and sister having a spat about a trivial domestic item. It was generally left to Maureen to put on the brave public face as her runaway husband played hookey with his loyal bunch of parasites much in the way he had at Zan's all those years before.

Except Maureen didn't have the patience of Arthur Beatty.

It was an on-again, off-again marriage, with Jimmy spending days or weeks away at work and/or play and Maureen, all too often at the end of her tether, changing the locks on the doors so he couldn't sneak back any time he felt like it. According to Jimmy she threatened to divorce him so many times she eventually just left their marriage licence with her solicitor.

Jimmy later admitted his problems ran deeper than merely having fun, telling Richard Green of the *Observer*, "Being on the road is such a lonely life. It's easy to think, 'I'll nip down to the bar and have a drink.' Before you know it, you've got a problem. I was drunk for a long time. The older you get, the longer it takes to get over the hangovers. Eventually your game starts to suffer."

I made an analogy between Jimmy and Elvis Presley at the beginning of the book. They were alike in more sense than one. Both teenage prodigies in their chosen fields, they went on to develop strong relationships with a closely-knit band of male friends that threatened their marriages. Elvis had the so-called Memphis Mafia, a group of men who all but moved in to his Graceland mansion with him. Jimmy had innumerable mates who called to whatever home he happened to be living in with Maureen at all hours of the day and night, much to her consternation.

"The relationship men have with their best mates has its own code," Jimmy maintained, "and most women never get to understand it at all. It's brought Maureen and me to the brink many many times."

Sometimes Maureen must have been tempted to have him listed under Missing Persons because he went AWOL so often. This happened when there were domestic crises, when she needed him to vet a house purchase, or simply because she felt a husband should be with his wife and a father with his children. Jimmy dearly wanted to be a family man, but however hard he tried something always seemed to get in the way – just like something always seemed to get in the way of him winning the World Championship (maybe it was the same thing: his flakiness.)

On one occasion when the *News of the World* got wind of the fact that Maureen had thrown Jimmy out, they found a model willing to give them a 'kiss and tell' scoop on Jimmy that would scupper the many sponsorship deals that had been lined up for him as well as his marriage. He was told in no uncertain terms by his management that he'd have to get Maureen to take him back by hook or by crook, even for a day, to kill the story. Neither could he enter the house by the front door because the press were parked there.

The situation appealed to Jimmy's sense of adventure and he made his way through many back gardens, clambering over fences and tiptoeing across lawns, into his house. He and Maureen put on sweet smiles and greeted the press like, as he put it, "a honeymoon couple swearing undying love". Afterwards she threw his most beloved cue out with the rubbish – which, as any snooker player will tell you, is akin to having a limb amputated (his mother subsequently retrieved it.)

Maureen sometimes found phone numbers of women in Jimmy's trousers when she was turning the pockets out to wash them. He pleaded that the numbers were slipped into them surreptitiously by fans and that he'd done nothing untoward with the said ladies, but Maureen refused to believe him. Sometimes she got a can of paint and scrawled the numbers on the walls to embarrass him.

* * *

As well as the wayward influence of Alex Higgins, Jimmy is also good friends with Rolling Stones legend Ronnie Wood. "We met at a school Nativity play," Ronnie recalls. "Our kids were in it and we were struggling to get our camcorders working. We recognised each other, got chatting and a couple of days later I called over to see how he'd got on. We had a drink and I ended up staying over Christmas." It sounds very Jimmy all right.

A lot of drinking went on during these rendezvous. In fact when Jimmy complained that there was no pub near his house, Ronnie solved the problem by putting one in the house itself!

Ronnie has always been there for Jimmy when he's had problems, and vice versa. "I'm as crap at music as he is at snooker," Jimmy joked, "so it's a good relationship."

Another Ronnie, O'Sullivan, sometimes joins them for fun and games. In his autobiography O'Sullivan writes about being at Wood's house in Kingston once with Jimmy when he spotted a guitar with a big hole in it. Wood told him Keith Richards put a pillow over it one night and shot it when he heard it belonged to Mick Jagger. Ronnie noticed loads of pillow feathers through the hole so he believed the story ... and decided to be nice to Richards the next time he met him.

Later that night Ronnie and Jimmy went to Wood's house to wind down after playing an exhibition match together. 'Jimmy and me were still in our dinner suits,' Ronnie wrote, 'somewhat the worse for wear and talking a load of crap to each other. We were telling each other what we were going to do in the coming season – if we managed to get our heads straight – but we were really just a couple of lunatics waiting for the next party.'

The following day Keith Richards visited and Ronnie and Jimmy played 11 frames for him. Jimmy made 6 centuries and Ronnie 5. I'm sure this is unparalleled in the game. It's a pity there were no television cameras there to capture it. Wrote Ronnie: 'I got a bigger buzz out of that than winning the World Championship. We were off our nuts.'

Maybe it helped that every 15 minutes Richards supplied them with a huge jug of vodka and orange. As Ronnie puts it, 'Even if we'd not been playing so brilliantly, in the state we were in we'd have thought we were.' Nobody mentioned the guitar with the feathers in it.

In Ronnie Wood's autobiography *Ronnie* (not to be confused with Ronnie O'Sullivan's one of the same name), the Rolling Stone tells many fond stories about his life on the razzle with Jimmy. At one point he mentions that he asked Jimmy to smash a few balls around a snooker table for background noise to one of the Rolling Stones's songs 'You Just Might Get To Like It' as he wanted that particular type of cacophony on the soundtrack. I'm sure this was a first for Jimmy – and rock music. 'Snooker Loopy' it was not.

In another chapter Wood reveals Jimmy almost caused a major marital spat between Ronnie and his then-wife Jo (the marriage collapsed in 2008 when Ronnie took up with a Russian girl young enough to be his grand-daughter) because he recorded one of Jimmy's Sheffield displays over his wedding tape to the horror of his missus.

A more tragic event occurred one morning when Ronnie and Jimmy, having been up all night playing snooker and partying in Wood's house were joined at breakfast time by Jo's father Michael, a lovely man who 'looked like Peter Ustinov, made architectural models including the Thames Flood Barrier, brought Lambrettas to the UK and had a Lambretta museum down in Devon'. Michael offered to cook breakfast for them, but they weren't hungry so the three of them just decided to have a laugh and joke around the table instead. The exertions proved too much for Michael, however. As Wood puts it, 'He joined in on the joke, had one last laugh and then he died in front of us.'

Alex Higgins, perhaps not surprisingly, often joined Jimmy and Ronnie in their madcap antics while hanging out at Wood's Kildare pad. In his book, Ronnie contends that Alex really always preferred horses to snooker players. This is how he puts it: 'He'd come into my room in the morning wearing a pair of women's tights and a little T-shirt, get into my bed with all the papers and tip sheets, and ask me which horse I liked in the 2.30 at Epsom. All I could do was lie there screaming, "What are you doing in bed next to me dressed in my wife's fucking tights?"'

One final anecdote in the book features Jimmy passing out after a party at Wood's house, lying in the studio at the bottom of Wood's garden all night as Maureen searched frustratedly for him. When she finally discovered him she grabbed Jimmy by the collar and roared at him as she dragged him across the lawn. Halfway back to the house Jimmy woke up. Amidst Maureen's tirade, all he could muster was, "What's for breakfast, love?" Wood watched the proceedings from a window in hysterics.

After his accountant informed him he'd blown something in the region of £3 million in his career, eventually Jimmy agreed with Maureen that his lifestyle couldn't go on forever. He joined both Alcoholics Anonymous and Gamblers Anonymous – even though it was difficult to be anonymous when you were Jimmy White. A lot of the money had gone on cards and horses as well as booze.

At the end of 1999 a book appeared called *Twelve Grand*. Written by Jonathan Rendall, it was about a guy who was given that amount by a London publisher and asked to gamble with it. Neat idea. Especially when it was set in Las Vegas and involved women, horses and drink.

Needless to say, Jimmy also cropped up. 'Ah, Jimmy White,' writes Randall. 'If you ever need some quick money, ask Jimmy for a game of cards. Poor, sweet Jimmy. I still had his phone number. 147147. Maximum break. "They can't take that away, can they?" Jimmy said. When Jimmy loses, a part of me bleeds. Just to think of Jimmy makes me smile.'

I couldn't have put it better myself.

Needless to say, such indulgences also had spillover effects on his game. As he lived, so he played. When Jimmy got back on the table, hungover and cash-strapped, he took on the kinds of shots that gave his diehard fans flutters of the heart.

A lot of times they came off, but when they didn't he lost matches to players who shouldn't even have been in the same building as him. This meant that Jimmy never had as much silverware in his cabinet as he should have, or wasn't as high in the computer rankings as his talent deserved. But each year at Sheffield he seemed to marshall extra strength and doing so well protected his ranking because double points were awarded for each match won in the World Championships. So even if he had a dreadful season and performed well there, he could comfortably stay in the elite top 16, or even, in the early 1990s, threaten the top 4.

Somehow his ranking and his marriage survived the carnage of Jimmy's wild recklessness. At least for now.

CRACKING THE NUGGET

AFTER JIMMY AND Ronnie Wood had palled up, Harvey Lisberg said to Jimmy, "I always thought of you being like the Rolling Stones. Davis is more like the Beatles." Personally I've always thought Davis was more like Cliff Richard.

Jimmy wrote his first book in 1988. It wasn't really the one we expected, i.e. tales of drink and drugs on the road, but rather the kind of thing you might have expected from Davis or Reardon: a how-to guide to snooker called *Jimmy White's Masterclass*.

Perhaps it was done in an attempt to tidy up his image. In it we get sentences like, 'Alcohol can be a pleasant form of relaxation, but keep it well away from a snooker table.' The words 'pot', 'kettle' and 'black' spring to mind.

Elsewhere we read, 'This wonderful game of snooker will degenerate back to the grimy halls it came from if we do not demand standards of etiquette from players at all levels.' All in all, it's quite sad to hear Jimmy (via his ghostwriter) espouse sentiments like this considering the fact that what his true fans always loved about him was his scallywag origins, or the fact that he cut his teeth (probably literally) when journeying from one 'grimy' hall to another.

Matters were somewhat more propitious on the table. Jimmy performed well in the Fidelity Unit Trusts International, his most satisfying match being against Willie Thorne in Round 5. He trailed 3-1, but took 3 frames on the bounce to lead for the first time before Thorne levelled with a break of 60. In the final frame shoot-out he had a pink for the match, but missed it. Thorne potted it, but couldn't get on the black, eventually leaving it for Jimmy in the middle pocket. In the next round he disposed of Barry West 5-2 and then beat Dean Reynolds 9-5 in the semi-final, but he collapsed against Davis in the final, going down miserably by 6 frames to 12.

Davis played out of his skin in that match, compiling 3 successive centuries in frames 9, 10 and 11. It was the first time he'd done that in competition. "I've never played better than that in my life," he said afterwards, "though Jimmy made it easy for me by giving me a lot of chances." It was the fourth time Jimmy had been beaten by Davis in a major final and it hurt. "He's not in a class of his own," he remarked afterwards, "and neither am I, but to beat him you have to be in top form."

As a consolation prize Jimmy won the LGE International in Hong Kong, defeating Neal Foulds 6-4 in the final. He'd actually led 5-0, fluking the black in the fifth frame to the delight of the crowd, before Foulds came back at him and nearly stole the match. This time Jimmy clung on.

In the BCE Canadian Masters that year Jimmy whitewashed Steve Longworth 5-0 in the opening round, thereby serving notice to all the other players that he meant business. But in the next round when his match with Dennis Taylor was squared at 3-3 you could see the tension etched onto his face. Jimmy eventually wrapped up the following two frames for victory, but remarked afterwards, "These short matches are brain damage to me". And to us, Jimmy. And to us.

That hurdle safely negotiated, he trounced Mike Hallett 9-2 in the semi-final, while Davis came through the other semi against Stephen Hendry. (Hendry hadn't yet learned how to beat Davis, but would soon.)

That left the stage set for yet another major final between the Nugget and the Whirlwind. Jimmy hadn't beaten Davis at all for two years, but saw him off here with a comfortable 9-4 margin, thereby ending a run of 22 ranking victories for Davis and giving him his heaviest beating ever in a final. "I owed him this one," Jimmy said afterwards, adding wryly, "In fact I think I owe him about 20."

He savoured the moment, as did any neutrals who liked to see other names on trophies besides that of the Ginger Magician. "The rubber band came off tonight," Davis declaimed rather enigmatically to the press after exiting the tournament.

It was Jimmy's first ranking tournament victory for 18 months, while he hadn't beaten Davis in a final since 1981 when he'd won the Northern Ireland Classic 11-9, so he had a point to prove.

In the Norwich Union Grand Prix, which was played in front of an elite audience in the luxurious Beach Plaza Hotel in Monte Carlo, Jimmy again faced

Davis in the final and there was even more drama here. It wasn't a ranking tournament and only eight players competed, but Jimmy fancied dealing Davis another bodyblow. Davis had beaten Jimmy in the final of the Fidelity Unit Trusts International not long before so it was 1-1. Who would prevail this time?

Jimmy went 4-1 up, but, as was to happen so often in his career, seemed uncomfortable to be ahead and started to make unforced errors. In the 8th frame he led by 55 points to 40 with just pink and black remaining, so Davis needed a snooker. He laid three good ones, but Jimmy got out of each of them in turn. Eventually Davis left a long pink for Jimmy. It was a tempter, but a bit in-offish, so Jimmy took his time over it. Eventually, being Jimmy, he decided to take it on. It proved to be a fatal decision. He potted the pink all right and for about five seconds the match was over. But then, as he feared, the cue ball agonisingly rolled its way back towards where he was standing and fell into the pocket.

It was re-spotted and Davis potted it along with the black to square the match. In the deciding frame Jimmy took a 41-25 point lead, but then got a horrendous kick on a pink and handed the initiative to Davis, which the Nugget gratefully grabbed with both hands. He made a 35 break which was enough for him to steal the match. Jimmy was inconsolable, saying, "Don't ask me what went wrong. I must have had that match won four times over."

Davis doubled his agony by remarking, "Jimmy should have put the boot in when I was there for the taking. He missed a big chance to score an important psychological victory." It was the story of so many of their encounters.

* * *

In the second round of the World Championships that year Jimmy was drawn against a promising young Scot called Stephen Hendry. Hendry had recently won the British Open and in some circles was being touted as the new Jimmy White. Still only a teenager, Hendry was already recognised as a possible future world champion, so Jimmy wasn't taking anything for granted. Hendry was actually bookies' favourite for the match, surprisingly in view of Jimmy's status in the game, though the youngster was already closing in on Davis's number one ranking spot (as indeed was Jimmy at this point of his career, though he never usurped it).

The first session was quickfire stuff with lots of big breaks. Hendry made a 78 in the first frame, but Jimmy then reeled off the next three in record time. He could have built an unassailable lead in this session, but failed to pot crunch balls in some of the succeeding frames and led just 5-3 overnight. He took the first frame the following morning, but then Hendry made a supersonic surge and took the next six frames to lead 9-6. Jimmy won the very important last frame of the session to trail by just two frames instead of a possible four going into the final day's play

The following morning began with an incident that was characteristic of Jimmy's integrity right through his career. He was snookered behind the brown at a crucial stage of the 17th frame. He played what appeared to be the perfect escape, but declared a foul on himself that nobody, including the referee, had seen, saying his sleeve had brushed a ball. That gesture of honesty resulted in him going three frames behind again. But now it was Jimmy's chance to shine and he reeled off four frames in a row to lead 11-10. Hendry then made a century, his third of the match, to level things.

11-11 and all to play for. Jimmy made a 64 break to inch ahead by 12 frames to 11 and looked set to seal the match in the next frame before breaking down on a 48 break. Hendry stepped up to the plate and forced things to a decider. In the last frame Jimmy was in the baulk area early on in the frame with the reds appetisingly set for the first player to get in. He played a brilliant cut on a red from 9 feet away to set himself up for a frame and match-winning 86 as the audience went wild.

It was an epic contest between two green baize gladiators, both playing fantastically at the same time. The commentators said it was a pity there had to be a loser, but I couldn't be this objective. I was dizzy with excitement that Jimmy had pulled off another close one. I'll never forget that magical Saturday morning. Perhaps the greatest tribute the BBC could pay to the match was that they let it eat into *Grandstand* for more than half an hour. Could there be a greater compliment than that? Could it be conceivable that snooker would (whisper it) be of passing interest to the soccer fraternity? Okay, so Gary Lineker used to make centuries at Willie Thorne's club in Leicester, but...

So many people flooded out of the Crucible when the match was over that the traffic in central Sheffield came to a standstill. The young pretender was defeated. Now for the current king to have his crown toppled. It looked like Jimmy's finest hour had come at last.

White breezed past Tony Knowles in the next round, but then met a resolute Terry Griffiths who didn't give an inch. At 11-13 down Jimmy played an excellent endgame to tie the 25th frame, but Griffiths got the re-spotted black and virtually killed off Jimmy's fighting spirit with that shot. He wasn't to win another frame and Griffiths made the final, only to be throttled 18-11 by Davis.

Soon afterwards Davis brought out a spoof book on snooker. Co-written with Geoff Atkinson, a TV producer and comedy writer who's worked with the likes of Rory Bremner and Mark Thomas, in it he cheekily sent himself up as a bore, but in doing so actually became anything but one. One imagines most of the gags were Atkinson's, but that's hardly relevant. Of Jimmy, Davis wrote, 'When he came on the scene I was pretty jealous of him. After all, he had a nickname at the time and I didn't. In fact after one tournament I went up to Jimmy and tried to pretend I didn't know he was called the Whirlwind. He said, "Hi Steve" and I said, "I didn't know you were called Whirlwind, Whirlwind," as casually as you like. That immediately let him know I was no mug.'

In the book Davis lists Jimmy's birth sign as 'Silk Cut', his favourite food as 'twenty Rothmans' and his hobby as 'Greek philosophy'. At the end of the book he tells us he consulted one of Jimmy's to help him write it. The title? *The Jimmy White Anthology of British Literature (previously published as* The Beano*).*

I caught up with Jimmy again in the Keadeen Hotel in 1989 as he was preparing for a match in the Irish Masters. He agreed to speak to me as he was practising on the hotel table. I sat in the room throwing questions at him as he played remarkable snooker, but just this once I wish he hadn't because he talked in that sepulchral drawl as he potted, and each time a ball slammed into one of the pockets it seemed to drown out his words. Many of them were lost to me afterwards when I played back the tape of our conversation. It was almost as if he hit the balls extra hard when he was avoiding questions he didn't like so I wouldn't hear the answers.

I repeated some questions I'd already asked him in our 1987 conversation. Why had he lost the 1984 final? "The semi-final against Kirk Stevens drained me. I had nothing left for Davis. He'd been in a final before and I hadn't. Maybe that was a factor. He stuffed me in the first session. I was struggling all the way after that."

Had he learned anything from the match? "Only that I'm fed up of losing to the Nugget." Point taken, but how would he contrive to stop it happening again? "I'm a different player at the moment, harder to beat. I'm concentrating more on my safety now. I have a more well-rounded game."

I put it to him that Clive Everton once said he didn't have a safety game. "That's not true. It's just that safety always bored me. I get no fulfilment from it. But if that's what it takes to win I'll develop it."

I then went on to ask him about his childhood. "I have three brothers and a sister. We've always been a very close-knit family, but none of the others play snooker." Did he feel he'd be successful as a child? "I'm still not successful! I won't say that until I'm world Number 1 and have won at Sheffield." Would beating Davis along the way be the icing on the cake? "Absolutely. If you don't get the Nugget it takes away from it a bit."

What did he think of Davis generally? "I respect him. He's very effective, and the hardest player in the game to beat, but I find his game boring." What about the 9-4 defeat of him in Canada – how sweet was that? "Very sweet. Not many players do him 9-4. I never expected it to be that comfortable."

How did he feel about beating Thorburn to win the Mercantile Credit Classic after that snooker! "I'm not known for my big breaks, but it proves I can do it when I want to. That shot gave me a lot of heart, especially after I lost so bad to him in the Goya." How did he lose that match after being seven frames up? "I lost it because I didn't think I could. That's always fatal." (A similar situation would come back to haunt him in the 1994 World final.)

Two days before I met him Jimmy had beaten Hendry 5-2 at Goffs. How did he feel about that match? "It was garbage," he declared. "Both of us played garbage. But sometimes you're just pleased to fall over the line even if the quality of the match is bad."

I asked him how he was feeling about his life in general. "Better," he said. "Having children cools you down. If this was two years ago I wouldn't even be practising now. I'd be in a club somewhere in Dublin, or at the track. The 80s was like one long party to me."

I mentioned the fact that Tony Meo had recently said he wasn't as 'slaphappy' as he used to be. "Maybe," he smiled, "we're all getting on." What about the comment he made to *Hot Press* magazine that his ambition was to "win a few world titles and then retire to breed dogs"?

"Did I say that?" he laughed. "If I did, I think different now. My gambling days are over."

Jimmy put down his cue for a few minutes and we talked about a recent bout with Dean Reynolds in which he'd led 6-3 but let Reynolds back to 8-8 before finishing him off. That gave him a fright. I wanted to know what he felt about another match between Terry Griffiths and Silvino Francisco which was being investigated by Scotland Yard for being fixed. "I know about the investigation, but I haven't seen the match so I can't comment. If anyone fixes a match they should be turfed out of the game."

We then talked about Maureen. He told me she didn't like the "politics and back-stabbing" in snooker so tended to stay away from the tournaments. What about the recent book he'd written called *Snooker Master Class*? I mentioned I was a bit surprised to see him coming out against players who drank. Was this not a bit rich from a player who lowered so many pints himself? "Maybe I'm qualified to talk about it for that very reason. I wouldn't want the younger players coming up to make the same mistakes I did," he said.

Jimmy returned to the table and I watched, fascinated, as he spun the cue around while lining up a shot. "Why do you do that?" I asked, having been vaguely aware of the mannerism for years. "I'm trying to find the grain," he said. As another ball slammed into a pocket I said, "The cue sounds tinny. Why is that?"

"How do you mean tinny?" he enquired. "The tip is a bit hard."

My nephew David was with me, taking the colours out of the pockets and respotting after Jimmy potted them. After the last red Jimmy potted the yellow, which David re-spotted. He potted it again and my nephew mistakenly took it out of the pocket. "It stays down," Jimmy said to him, momentarily petulant. I mentioned to him that he'd developed a red off a red a few shots before, something Eddie Charlton said a player should never do. "What would Eddie Charlton know?" he laughed, and the atmosphere relaxed again.

I was curious to know how his life had changed since he joined Barry Hearn's Matchroom stable. "It hasn't changed at all. How do you mean?" I wondered if it hadn't taken the sting off his rivalry with Davis, another Hearn client. "It makes it worse!" he insisted. I put it to him that Hearn once said Jimmy was more of an exhibitionist than a matchroom player. "That's bullshit," he said. "Like I told you, I can play safety now if I have to. If someone puts me on the back cushion, I'll put them on the back cushion."

We talked about the days with Dodgy Bob in the taxi. Had he ever got close to violence in some of the dives they went to? "There were nights when I felt it was in the air," he admitted. Was he ever afraid of having his thumbs broken, like the character Paul Newman played in *The Hustler*? "That's my favourite movie of all time," he said, avoiding the question.

What did he admire most about *The Hustler*? "I liked when Fast Eddie said, 'I can play this game the way nobody's ever played it before.'"

Did he feel that way about his own game? "We've talked about how people say I copied Alex, but he knows I have my own style. I'd like to think I play the game the hard way."

Is that the only way to play it? "No, but if you try to take too many shortcuts you're only fooling yourself."

I mentioned a shot he played against Reynolds when the red was on a cushion a quarter of the way down the table and the white in the middle of the table. He'd cut the red into the yellow pocket, an almost impossible angle. I ventured that it was the most brilliant shot I'd ever seen. "I must have won that frame," he said, smiling. In actual fact I couldn't remember if he had. That was the thing with Jimmy. He was the best plain ball potter in the game, but sometimes he didn't string enough great pots together to secure a frame.

So what of the future? "The World (Championship) is coming up after this tournament. That's my priority now, to get a good run in that." And that would mean defeating Davis at the Crucible.

We shook hands again as his minders closed around him. As he went to leave, who appeared at the door but Alex Higgins. The pair of them were obviously going off somewhere together, probably to the races (so much for his gambling days being over). I couldn't resist asking Alex about his 1982 match with Jimmy at Sheffield, in particular the break of 69 in the 30th frame. He was delighted that someone was still talking about it. "I knew I couldn't miss or I was dead," he beamed. I hat concentrated me.

Jimmy looked unimpressed. I asked him if he thought Alex could do the business that year at Sheffield. "No," he droned, "because I'll be doing the business at Sheffield."

Higgins couldn't have 'done the business' that year as things worked out because he was knocked out of the World Championships at the qualifying stage by Darren Morgan. But he continued to grab headlines for all the wrong reasons in the coming years. In 1990 at the Team World Cup he had a furious row with Dennis Taylor after which Higgins is alleged to have threatened Taylor's life. "I come from Coalisland," Alex supposedly said, "and the next time you're in Northern Ireland I'll have you shot."

Higgins denied saying these words. He claimed the actual words he used were, "If I had a gun in my hands I'd blow your brains out."

A fortnight later the pair faced each other in the Benson & Hedges Irish Masters quarter-final. I was slated to interview Jimmy that day, but he cried off. "I'll be watching the Match of the Century," he told me. In fact he commentated on it on television. It was the first time I'd ever heard him in the commentary box. But the match was an anti-climax. Taylor won it easily by 5 frames to 2.

The following month Higgins went out of the 1990 World Championships in the first round, losing 10-5 to Steve James. He seemed to twig this was the end for him and sat in his chair after the match finished, refusing to vacate the arena. An aerial camera shot of him sitting there drunk on vodka is a poignant coda to the Hurricane's career. As Higgins finally stood up to leave he ripped the head off a toy leprechaun he had brought with him as a good luck mascot. He also tore off a bracelet he was wearing which had been given to him by his then girlfriend Siobhan Kidd.

On his way to the press conference afterwards he punched the WPBSA press officer Colin Randle for no apparent reason. At the press conference itself he railed against corruption in snooker and announced his retirement form the game with the immortal words, "You can shove snooker up your jacksey." He threatened to 'blow the lid' on the game, but as Clive Everton observed wryly, "Alex *is* the lid."

In 1989 at Sheffield Jimmy beat Dene O'Kane 10-5 in the opening round before edging John Virgo out 13-12 in a second round thriller. At 12-11 Virgo showed White-like integrity in declaring a foul on himself that the referee hadn't seen and Jimmy stepped up to the table to take the frame. Having got out of jail his tail was up and he made a 61 in the 25th and final frame to book his place in the quarter-finals.

Before the shoot-out and the customary handshake Jimmy said to Virgo, "There must be an easier way to make a living than this!" Once more he prepared to walk the precipice that was his life in snooker.

Virgo tapped into the core of Jimmy's highly-strung temperament: "That continuous fiddling with his bow tie is a nervous habit," he believes, "and so too, in my opinion, is the frantic haste with which he often plays. He may look cool and composed, but I remember him diving out to the Gents during a final with Steve Davis and just standing there shaking like a leaf."

Maybe such nervousness was the cause of Jimmy's 13-7 quarter-final defeat to John Parrott. That was the year Parrott was slaughtered 18-3 in the final by Davis, a scoreline that haunted him and probably acted as a catalyst to his great start against Jimmy at the same stage of the tournament the following year. He didn't want to see history repeat itself. It was confirmation of Davis's domination of the game, and the decade, though Parrott's concentration was no doubt upset by the Hillsborough tragedy that had taken place just three miles away on the opening day of the final, a huge number of soccer supporters, most of whome hailed from Parrotts's home city of Liverpool being crushed to death after a stand collapsed before the FA Cup semi-final between Liverpool and Nottingham Forest.

1989 ended on a high note for Jimmy when he trounced Parrott 18-9 in the final of the Everest World Matchplay Championship. He took that form into the 1990 World Championships, playing some of his best snooker at Sheffield that year. In reaching the final he hardly had to exert himself, disposing of Danny Fowler 10-4 in the first round, then John Virgo 13-6 and Terry Griffiths 13-5. In the semi-final he met Davis. Most people expected Jimmy to lose as he'd never beaten him at this venue before, but Jimmy played like God to knock Davis out 16-14. It was the first time in four years Davis had been beaten in the Crucible, having been world champion in 1987, 1988 and 1989. Davis led 8-6 after the second session, but Jimmy won the third 7-1 to set himself up for victory with a dazzling display of potting. Davis graciously applauded Jimmy as he wrapped things up. Maybe he knew he'd finally overcome that mental block that dogged him for a decade now. The guard had changed. Jimmy's victory spelt the end of Davis's supremacy in the game, although it wasn't to usher in a period of White domination. Instead we entered what we might call the 'Hendry Decade'.

Journalist Eamon Dunphy described what happened in the *Sunday Independent*: 'Jimmy never lacked courage, but this week he discovered common sense. Playing Davis at the Crucible, the rule was you got one chance in each frame – if you were lucky. If you failed, he crucified you. Slowly. Watching from your seat he looked invulnerable. Despair settled in your gut. Doubts infected your spirit. The next time you got to the table, you knew the bastard was waiting like a vulture to feast on any error. That was pressure. He could break you just by sitting there impassively, waiting.' But Jimmy had withstood the heat in this most turbulent of pressure cookers.

The only problem was he'd beaten Davis in the semi-final, not the final. Sadly for Jimmy, his overcoming of one Crucible curse hurled him headlong into the arms of another. His next opponent was the man he'd beaten in the second round in 1988, the new shining light in the game, Stephen Hendry. That season Hendry had already won the British Open, the Dubai Classic, the Stormseal UK Championship and the Scottish Masters, mauling Terry Griffiths 10-1 in the final of the latter. En route to the World final he'd sent four good players packing: Alain Robidoux, Tony Drago, Darren Morgan and John Parrott. He expected to meet Davis in the final (after all he'd been in every final since 1982), but now that Jimmy had knocked the Nugget out there had to be a new name on the trophy.

There was, but it wasn't Jimmy's. He had been Hendry's hero as a child, but in this contest there was no nostalgia. Jimmy got his nose in front at 2-1, but never led again during the whole match. He levelled at 5-5, but Hendry held a 9-7 overnight lead, taking the last frame of the session with a crucial century. The next morning the teenager won the first four frames to move 13-7 ahead. There was nowhere for Jimmy to hide now. He got back to 10-14 and 11-15, but he needed one of his famous surges and it didn't come. Hendry froze Jimmy out by 18 frames to 12 to become the youngest world champion in history at 21 years and 3 months. He was the first Scot to lift the trophy since Roger Donaldson in 1950.

Jimmy knew he'd been outplayed. His safety wasn't what it needed to be against such a high scorer. This, his second World final defeat, wasn't a match he let slip away; the better player simply outshone him.

The young Jimmy White: Hot property in more ways than one, after turning professional in 1981 having won the World Amateur Championship.

Ghost-faced Jimmy prepares to take on Alex 'Hurricane' Higgins in the 1982 world semi-final, a match which has gone down in Crucible history as one of the finest ever seen there.

Jimmy takes on Steve Davis in the 1984 World final, a match which defined the rivalry between the pair for the new generation of snooker players weaned on the sport's glamorous TV scheduling.

Off the table Jimmy looks as tense beside Steve Davis as he usually was on it.

Sharing the glory of winning the 1984 World Hofmeister doubles with partner and chief troublemaker Alex Higgins.

With Maureen. Their relationship was as firey as any of the great love stories, but they were most often compared to screen idols Elizabeth Taylor and Richard Burton, probably because Jimmy, like Richard, could go missing on the razzle for days.

Fags and booze often combined with a third vice – gambling.

Having a chuckle with Alex Higgins. The pair were often inseparable, often raucous, and almost always laughing.

Showing off the World Masters trophy with proud father, Tommy.

With a very young Stephen Hendry and women's world champion Mandy Fisher at the 1991 Masters. Note the outlandish attire all round.

Jimmy became only the second man to make a Sheffield maximum in 1992 during his 10-4 first round win over Tony Drago.

In the 1992 final against Stephen Hendry, Jimmy led 14-8 and was a red and colour away from winning the next frame, but Hendry pulled off an astonishing turnaround to win 18-14, winning ten frames in a row.

Jimmy's early baldness saw him attempt to cover it up by undergoing an operation to cure it which saw a piece of plastic inserted under his scalp. But the procedure went wrong and he suffered swelling and a lot of pain, forcing him to miss tournaments as a result.

The closest Jimmy ever got to the World Championship trophy: before the 1994 final in which he lost 18-17 to Hendry to lose his fifth final in a row and sixth overall.

In 1998 Jimmy finally defeated Stephen Hendry at the World Championships, but then ran into 'Rocket' Ronnie O'Sullivan in the quarter-finals and lost 13-7.

Practice was never Jimmy's strong point. He was a man blessed with so much natural cue talent, potting ability, touch and ball skills.

Jimmy compiles another century break after finding himself in amongst the balls against Matthews Stevens in the 2000 Masters quarter-finals, but the Welshman went on to win the tournament…

… and Jimmy lost at the same stage of the World Championships to the same opponent that season.

DO YOU HAVE THE BALLS TO JOIN IN?

ON JUNE 9 GET YOUR KIT ON AND HELP US RAISE MONEY TO FIGHT MALE CANCER.

To pledge money or for more information call 0906 3022 502 (Calls cost 50p per minute)

Following his own cancer scare and the death of his mother and brother, Jimmy joined in Everyman's 2000 campaign alongside many of Britain's sporting heroes. The photograph, taken by Lord Lichfield, features (L-R) footballers Les Ferdinand and David Ginola, cricketer Phil Tufnell, rugby player Lawrence Dallaglio, jockey Richard Dunwoody, athlete John Regis, Jimmy, TV presenter Gabby Yorath (now Logan) and rugby player Brian Moore.

Jimmy's fans are renowned for their incredible support of their hero. Here Dominic Dale covers his ears to keep out the ferocity of their welcome for their hero as Jimmy enters the arena at the World Championships in 2002 for their first round match. It was all too much for Dale. Jimmy triumphed 10-2.

From left, James Wattana, Jimmy, Shokat Ali, Ken Doherty, Mark Williams, Stephen Hendry and China's Ding Junhui pose at a floating Chinese restaurant in Hong Kong to promote the first ever Euro-Asia Snooker Masters Challenge in August 2003.

Jimmy, in typically debonair waistcoat, pots another ball with one of his favourite implements, the rest, during the 2004 Masters.

In 2004, Jimmy won the Players Championship, his 10th ranking event, 12 seasons after his last such victory. Defeating Paul Hunter 9-7 in the final.

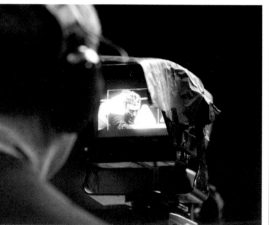

Under the watch of television cameras Jimmy plays a shot on the way to lifting the 2004 Players Championship. He has been used to living with such intense scrutiny throughout his career both on and off the table.

As well as winning the Players Championship, Jimmy just missed out on another ranking final in 2004, losing the Masters semi-final 6-4 to Ronnie O'Sullivan.

Watching as Barry Pinches knocks him out of the 2004 World Championships 10-8 in the first round. Snooker is a cruel game. Players remain helpless in their seats and watch as their opponents pounce on their mistakes.

Keeping Sky Sports presenter Dave Clark entertained at the Premier League event in Colchester in January 2005.

Carrying son Tommy, the new James Brown (as Jimmy renamed himself) is interviewed after beating Mark Williams in the Masters quarter-finals in 2005.

Jimmy makes his usual gladiatorial entrance before his Masters semi-final in 2005. He lost 6-1 to Ronnie O'Sullivan.

Jimmy's cheeky smile still endears him to thousands of devoted fans.

Sharing a joke with John Higgins in 2005.

Shaking hands with Matthew Stevens before losing 13-5 in the second round at Sheffield in 2005; to date Jimmy's last appearance in the World Championships.

Suffering in going down to defeat once again, this time 6-3 to John Higgins in the Saga Insurance Masters in January 2006.

Jimmy enters the auditorium at the 2007 Saga Insurance Masters to the acclaim of his many, and long-suffering, fans. He has been the most popular individual sportsman in the UK for nearly 30 years. But could a spell in ITV's reality jungle propel him back to the forefront of the nation's minds?

The spoils of war: Jimmy finished as runner-up in the Betfred.com Premier League in 2006, receiving a very tidy cheque as his prize.

ALWAYS THE BRIDESMAID

THE 1990/91 SEASON was a bumper one for Jimmy. He bagged the 555 World Series Challenge by thumping James Wattana 9-3, following that up with a victory over John Parrott in the final of the Humo Belgian Masters. He had a heartbreaker in the Rothmans Grand Prix where he looked set to make the final, but lost on the last ball of the last frame of the semi-final to a doughty Nigel Bond. He played well enough to win this match, but in the end it was Bond who had the steadier nerve to sink what was ultimately a pretty simple black after a loose safety by Jimmy.

A purple patch followed that setback as he won the Coalite World Matchplay, pulverising Hendry 18-9 in the final. He then dismissed the young Scot again soon afterwards by the resounding score of 10-4 in the final of the Mercantile Credit Classic. If that wasn't enough, he also won the Mita World Masters, brushing Tony Drago aside 10-6 in the final.

Three consecutive victories were followed by three semi-final disappointments in a row. Hendry got his revenge in the Benson & Hedges Masters, crushing Jimmy 6-1 in the semi-final. In the Pearl Assurance British Open he got to the semi-final only to be denied by Gary Wilkinson in another match that went the distance, Jimmy bowing out 8-9. Davis also knocked him out of the Benson & Hedges Masters semi-final by the odd frame at 6-5, which left only the World Championship left to play. He went into the tournament in white-hot form. Could this be the year?

Jimmy breezed through the first round, beating Nick Dyson 10-3. The second round match against Neal Foulds went to 12-12. I was seriously considering visiting the Coronary Care Unit of my local hospital during the last frame, but Jimmy edged it. Having overcome this obstacle it was business as usual against Wilkinson in the quarter-finals, Jimmy paralysing him 13-3. In the semi-final he expected to meet Hendry, but Steve James had knocked him out in a shock result in the other half of the draw. Jimmy didn't have too many problems against James, winning 16-9. John Parrott would be his opponent in the final. Parrott had beaten Davis 16-10 in the semi-finals, thereby regaining his self-respect after Davis's 18-3 slaughter of him at the same venue two years previously.

Sadly for Jimmy, this final was over almost as soon as it began. From the moment Parrott picked out a plant with his very first shot the jovial Liverpudlian never looked back. He raced into a 7-0 lead in the first session, as Davis had in his 1984 final against Jimmy. Jimmy fought bravely, but never really managed to get into the match. The seven frames were won in little more than an hour's playing time. That demonstrated how much it was one-way traffic. Parrott racked up a total of 634 points in these frames compared to a miserable 80 from Jimmy. It was Christians and Lions fare.

Having to play Jimmy at the Crucible, Parrott remarked, "was a bit like Liverpool playing at Arsenal." It was like a home game for Jimmy. He had the extra man in the crowd – or several hundred extra men. Parrott knew he had to fight the crowd as well as Jimmy. "If I make a century I get a polite clap. All Jimmy has to do is break off for the roof to cave in with the roars." But the roars meant little on this occasion.

Parrott won a few frames on the black to kill Jimmy's spirit every time he started a resurgence. He couldn't quite shake him off, but neither could Jimmy make any serious inroads into the deficit. Parrott lead 11-5 overnight. Jimmy won the first two frames the next day, but then Parrott landed another sucker punch, taking the 19th frame by just one point on the black. Jimmy got it back to 12-8, and should have gone 12-9, but a mistake on the blue cost him the frame and effectively the match. It was all a bit like watching somebody being slowly strangled.

The early seven-frame deficit was insurmountable and that was the margin he eventually lost by; 18-11 to the canny scouser.

Parrott was wound up like an elastic band for the match. 'I can't remember a single face in the audience,' he wrote in his autobiography, 'or even what the referee looked like. I was so locked into the game, all I was aware of were the balls on the table.'

His motivation was increased as the result of a lengthy conversation he'd had shortly beforehand with John Spencer one night in, of all places, an Irish pub. It was here Spencer told Parrott, who'd lost 18-3 to Davis in the previous year's final, as mentioned, that he seemed to have a Sheffield mental block and if he could get over that he could beat anyone. Parrott took this on board and beat Davis in the semi-final before his match with Jimmy. It was that victory which really gave him the belief in himself that he could go all the way. Ironically, after Jimmy had lost the final, Spencer felt guilty about the advice he gave Parrott because he had so much affection for the Whirlwind. In fact there was no player he'd like to have seen win at Sheffield more. But when he'd spoken to Parrott he wasn't to know it would be Jimmy he would defeat in the final.

What went wrong for Jimmy? In a word: preparation. Future world champion Ronnie O'Sullivan went to Sheffield to see the match as a 15-year-old boy and got something of a shock. He was amazed both at the number of hangers-on that Jimmy had, and also their cockiness. "Jimmy's got this one in the bag," they chirped over beers, "and we're going to be celebrating." This was before the match even started. We all like admirers, but Jimmy collected so many Yes-men around him it was as if he needed excessive praise to bolster his self-image. He was shy on the table and taciturn in interviews but full of a kind of macho posturing when among his own. The pity was that they were filling him up with excessive notions of his chances because they weren't *au fait* with the inside track of the game. He needed to be confronted with harsher truths from a strict coach or manager, but that would have been too much like being back at school again.

There were always too many people pulling out of Jimmy, hangers-on in his dressing room telling him matches were foregone conclusions before the off. They should have realised Parrott was always a tough nut to crack. He wasn't regarded as a genius, but he was solid as a rock and rarely missed easy shots. What you got from him you earned. Neither should anyone have forgotten that he put Jimmy out of Sheffield two years before.

Jimmy, unfortunately, believed his publicity. He became intoxicated with the perfume of flattery. Parrott became a soft touch to him in his mind. Jimmy took the match for granted and had the rug pulled from under his feet. Afterwards he was as sick as another kind of parrot.

* * *

Jimmy was so ubiquitous on television at this point of his career he even managed to engage the attentions of visiting American stand-up comedian Bill Hicks, who featured him in an act he gave at the Oxford Playhouse. "Who is this Jimmy White?" he asked, feigning bewilderment. "The last time I was here I turned on the TV and there he was. Nine months earlier the last thing I saw when I left the hotel room – Jimmy fucking White. Does this guy not have a home life or something? Let's get him home. Let's iron that vest!"

Many people's problem at this time (mine included) was that Jimmy simply wasn't shown enough on TV. It was often the plough-horses of the game who got on the prime time slots. If you didn't have satellite, or couldn't afford to go to the matches, you were dependent on late night highlights where a dramatic match was shoehorned into a short programme that had to skip a lot of frames to fit into the slot.

I didn't have teletext, so often had to ring up the sports departments of newspapers to get updates. If I wasn't near a phone I chewed my fingernails, sometimes till they bled. If I was away on holidays with Mary I tried to ensure the room had got satellite TV. She used to joke that if we ever divorced she'd cite Jimmy as co-respondent. He seemed to overshadow everything we did in some way or another.

"Why don't you follow people who win?" she asked me once, like Hugo. I told her Jimmy had a proud track record of nine ranking titles and numerous other tournament wins. It was only Sheffield that was the bogey. But his failure to win a World title would come to be what people remembered about Jimmy, not his genius. It was, after all, the centre stage, the place where his dream would hopefully one day be unveiled – maybe even on his birthday. That would surely seal the fairytale and silence his critics. But first he had to change his tactics.

Jimmy needed unpredictability, I told her. He got bored when things were too easy. But then he created challenges for himself that he couldn't always meet and suddenly what had been boring a few minutes before was now beyond him. He found himself flying blind into self-imposed problems and sometimes panicked as a result. His detractors said he choked, or lost his bottle, but it was much more complicated than that. He was fighting the enemy within as he created a new game that was like a hall of mirrors, a Russian doll shedding its layers so much that the smallest one wasn't even visible.

This was obtuse, even Kafkaesque. In snooker terms what it meant was that Jimmy was leading a frame by twentysomething points and there was one red left on the table. Potting it meant the other guy needed snookers, but it was along the cushion. Cuter players would send it round the table and leave the white stuck to the black. Not Jimmy. He had to take it on. His fans, and his reputation, demanded this of him. The added pressure meant he couldn't roll it in like he did in practice, but hitting it harder meant it was likely to jaw. Parrott or Ebdon seemed to have a facility for playing this shot in such a way that even if they missed it, it ran safe. With Jimmy it always seemed to stay on the hole. So now he'd stuck his opponent up. You can guess the rest. Another frame had gone west, another nail in his coffin. These frames are always the hardest to take. They fill the winner with adrenalin and the loser with dread. The heart goes out of him. You can almost bet on him to lose the next one as well, or the next few. Matches turn on shots like that. And they're preventable.

1992 was as interesting a year for Jimmy as 1982 had been. (He shone particularly in those years where his age reached a new decade: 20 and now 30.) He won both the British and European Open, the Rothman's Grand Prix and the UK Championship.

He'd begun the 1991/2 season well, gaining some sort of revenge over Parrott to win the UK Open 16-13 in the final. In the final of the European Open he had even less trouble against Mark Johnston-Allen, virtually mugging him at 9-3. In the Pearl Assurance British Open he won a very tight match against Davis in the semi-finals 9-8 before meeting James Wattana in the final. It was a surreal tournament for Wattana because he'd entered his last 16 match with Tony Drago after being informed his father had just been shot in Bangkok. He compiled a maximum break in that match (amazingly under the circumstances), but when he came off the table, having won 5-1, he learned his father had died. Wattana opted to stay in the tournament and reached the final, but Jimmy raced into a 7-0 lead. Wattana fought back bravely, but Jimmy held his nerve to finally win 10-7.

He was prouder of the way he played in the UK Championship, where he beat Parrott 16-9 in the final, than anything he did before or since. "I felt I could pot anything from anywhere," he said after his victory. It certainly looked like it.

He was also in sizzling form in Sheffield that year, even managing a maximum en route to his fourth world final. The break took place during his first round tie with his friend Tony Drago. He was leading 8-4 at the time, but he'd been 8-2 up, so wanted to re-assert himself in the match. It was after cannoning into the pack after the fifth black that he started to think the maximum could be on. But after he potted the tenth one he missed the angle to go into the pack, hitting the pink instead. He now had to play a red that was in the baulk area. In retrospect this worked in his favour as it got it out of the way. It wasn't too difficult a cut, but playing a ball ten feet away and coming back to land perfectly on the black was a bit rich. Many would have opted against it and played safe. Not Jimmy. He nailed it and after that it was plain sailing apart from nearly missing the green. He punched the air when the 36th ball went down. It was unusual for Jimmy to show any emotion at all, but you knew he would this time. Drago was delighted for him, as were the crowd. The arena erupted into raucous cheers. He'd just earned £100,000 for making a 147 and all but booked himself a place in the next round. After the next frame, he'd done precisely that.

An interviewer asked him about the "new and improved" Jimmy White, who'd cut out the late nights and the reckless living. When he asked him how long he'd been off the booze, Jimmy replied (á la George Best), "That's easy. 27 days, 3 hours and 21 minutes."

Not too many people were surprised that Jimmy made the World final once again, but when he went 12-6 up against Stephen Hendry in the late afternoon of the first session a hush went around the auditorium.

Jimmy also led 14-8, but Hendry nicked the last two frames of the session to go just 14-10 down. In retrospect this was massive as 16-8 would have been an unassailable lead. Hendry was well aware of Jimmy's brittle temperament when someone was coming back at him. He told himself that if he could win three of the first four frames that night he would be only two frames behind at 15-13. At 14-9, Jimmy was 52 points ahead when Hendry pounced, clearing the table to reduce his deficit to just four frames going into the final session rather than the expected six. This changed the complexion of the rest of the evening significantly.

A funny thing happened to me in the course of that match. Jimmy was leading 14-8 when the phone rang. It was an editor from a Dublin paper, a man I never heard from before or since, who asked me to do an article for him on musicians who had never performed in Ireland. A weird idea at a weird time, but what the hell, it was work so I said I'd do it. Jimmy was so far ahead there was no way Hendry could catch him now. This final was almost getting boring.

I went down to a pub to write out some notes on the article and have a meal. I hadn't been able to eat anything at lunchtime as I watched Jimmy building that big lead, but now my appetite was coming back. Before the food came I was watching the match on the pub television, but I had to go over to a table with my tray. The TV set wasn't visible from where I was now sitting. I heard some wild cheering over the next ten or fifteen minutes and presumed it was for Jimmy. I knew they had two frames left to play before the interval. With luck the score could be 16-8: an uncatchable lead. I found myself almost wishing Hendry would win one of them to make it a bit more dramatic. To this day I blame that editor for the fact that Jimmy lost the match. I needed to be there watching him for him to produce his best.

At 14-9 up, Jimmy led by 42 points, but then missed a red with the rest. He didn't usually miss with this implement. One's memory went back to the fatal moment in 1982 when he had, though, against Higgins. On that occasion the balls weren't ideally placed for a clearance and neither were they here, but Hendry still did the necessary, just as Higgins had. What should have been 15-9 in Jimmy's favour was now just 14-10. Game on.

Jimmy also blew the first frame of the evening when he only needed a red to leave Hendry needing two snookers. It wasn't an unduly difficult shot, but his nerves were shot. In such situations anything can be missed. Jimmy knew Hendry was on the prowl and the Scot took the frame and closed the gap to three. The next one was also close, but Hendry shaved it on the pink. In the following frame

Jimmy went in-off after screwing into the pack. It looked like somebody up there didn't like him.

Hendry's confidence grew with every frame. I felt if he got level Jimmy was probably dead. I was down on my knees at the TV set begging him to pinch just one frame of the session. But he didn't. Hendry got to level-pegging and now the writing was most definitely on the wall. Could Jimmy rally?

There were, to be sure, great comebacks in the history of snooker. Taylor against Davis in the 1985 World final, or the equally dramatic one where Higgins came back from 7-0 against Davis in the 1983 Coral final to nick the match 16-15. I also remembered being at Goffs one night where Higgins trailed Cliff Thorburn 4-0 and came back to win 5-4. But had Jimmy ever performed a Houdini act like this? None sprang to mind. All I could think of were gallant defeats. This match, for so long a guaranteed cert, was shaping up to being an ungallant one.

Jimmy had entranced us all exactly ten years before when he went toe to toe against Higgins in the semi-final. He would have been a world champion at 20 then if he'd beaten Higgins and Reardon. But he didn't. Were we about to see a re-run of that disaster?

Hendry suddenly became psychological favourite and the betting odds changed. The match was now effectively a best of nine. As Jimmy put it, "Stephen went from a position of being dead and buried to being very much alive and kicking."

Before the match began if he was asked would he settle for a 14-14 scoreline heading into the last session Jimmy would have been over the moon. But now the initiative was with Hendry.

As they got ready for the last session I got to thinking maybe some things were destined not to happen in sport. Ilie Nastase not winning Wimbledon. George Best or Ian Rush not getting to play in a World Cup. These things were destined not to happen, and the more you tried to fight that destiny the more you crucified yourself. Far better to just take whatever gravy there was and bend the knee, because otherwise you were just postponing the inevitable.

When the final session began Jimmy looked edgy. So what else was new? But Hendry had a determined look on his face. I recalled the time he came from 1-8 down against Mike Hallett to win 10-9. Hallett went for a pint with Hendry after that match. Would Hendry have gone with Hallett if the situation had been reversed? I doubted it. It was the killer streak thing again. Hendry never gave up on a frame until the referee started re-racking the balls. That was what made a champion. If Jimmy had been 14-8 behind he would already have been thinking of the long trip up the M1.

I felt somebody needed to give Jimmy a sound thrashing. I couldn't think of any other player who seemed to be letting a world title slip away from him this lamely. He wasn't just being outplayed, he was being out-thought, out-psyched. His stubbornness wouldn't let him change his strategy, or rather lack of one. There was no Plan B. I finally realised what people meant when they said he was unmanageable. It wasn't just the late nights or the mad lifestyle. It was his failure to listen to anyone who said he didn't adapt his game to suit the emergency of the moment.

I once put it to Jimmy that the frame of snooker was really a frame of mind. He agreed. After Hendry started to come back at him in 1992 he panicked. It was like watching the Goya Final of 1985 all over again. He refused to steady the ship, instead blithely carrying on trying to pot his way back into the ascendancy. It wasn't as if Hendry was doing anything brilliant. He just kept chipping away at the lead and watching Jimmy self-destruct. Every time Jimmy got in he only made small breaks. You could bet on him to take on and miss the awkward balls. Somebody needed to take him aside and tell him to make Hendry work harder for it. He wanted to get on a charge again, but that was never going to happen. If this match was going to be won it was going to be won by grinding. And that Jimmy could never do.

When they came back after the final interval Hendry surged ahead. 15-14 became 16-14. Jimmy was on the road to Gethsemane. You felt that now he wanted to be out of the arena with or without the trophy. Hendry was smelling blood everywhere, almost licking his lips the way Davis did, like a cat after a mouse. The final score, 18-14 to Hendry, had a terrible sense of inevitability about it.

Afterwards Jimmy said, "I can't feel gutted. Stephen played like God."

I didn't really agree. People only play as well as you let them. Every time Hendry came to the table it seemed like Jimmy had left him a picnic. In any break the first red is usually the hardest shot. Because Jimmy played such an open game, that red was often left in the open for Hendry. And of course the Scot had infinitely more table time than Jimmy as the match went on so it gave him a chance to get his rhythm going.

The defeat hurt me to the quick.

English essayist William Hazlitt wrote, 'The greatest reversals of fortune are the most easily borne, from a sort of dignity belonging to them.' Jimmy personified the veracity of that dictum. He'd been beaten not necessarily by a better player but by someone who lived on the planet Earth, who was pragmatic. It was a bit like the record producer who said to Leonard Cohen once, "We know you're great, Lennie, but are you any good?" What point was there possessing genius if he didn't have street suss?

Jimmy reached the World final again in 1993. Guess who he was up against? Stephen Gordon Henry. Even before this match began you felt there could only be one winner. You felt if Hendry got any kind of a lead going he'd steamroller Jimmy.

Well he did – and he did. The final score was 18-5, Hendry winning with a session to spare. In fact his whole Sheffield campaign that year had been something of a stroll. His aggregate frame score was 70 for and 25 against: a staggering statistic. Every time Jimmy bent down to take a shot you could almost see him thinking about the year before when he'd let such a big lead slip. Hendry made eight centuries in the match. The Whirlwind had been humbled in the most public fashion. I wondered if Jimmy would be able to cope with such crushing disappointment. He clearly hadn't been able to put the mental anguish of letting the previous season's big lead slide away from him.

Hendry had had a tough 1992/93 season. Before playing in the Grand Prix he received death threats from a woman who wrote a play with the Agatha Christie style title of *Death in the Billiard Room* and sent it to him. In her story Hendry is murdered at the end. The Scot fell at the first hurdle in this tournament, his nerves rattled, but he went on to win subsequent ones, telling us all we need to know about the man's inner steel.

Was this the reason why Hendry was world champion four years in succession from 1992 to 1995? It seemed to me it was indicative of the reason why Jimmy White was so often the bridesmaid.

* * *

On 23 January 1994, Maureen announced that her marriage to Jimmy was over. The main reason she gave was the company he kept, what she called his "scummy hangers-on". "Jimmy has always been one of the lads," she complained. "He's always needed to be in a gang. He's never really grown up. His best friend is Ronnie Wood. They love doing wild things together. But there are others around too, less than savoury characters."

Wood himself admitted that Jimmy surrounded himself with lowlifes. "I used to join him and the rest of the blokes for drinks," he said once, "and suddenly he'd announce he was playing a match in a couple of hours. I'd be horrified. If I'd known I'd have made sure he was in bed, but the other blokes didn't seem to care. Jimmy was led on because he was so nice."

Jimmy moved into a rented house near his family home in Surrey, momentarily shaking off the image of the dad who enjoyed country walks and Sunday roasts with his wife and children. But Maureen didn't formally divorce him at this point. They still had strong feelings for each other and Jimmy continued to see his children. They were torn in their affections and loyalties. It was hard to kick off the vestiges of their tortuous relationship, but for Maureen things couldn't have continued as they were. She needed some still point in her life.

Jimmy, on the contrary, seemed to thrive on the chaos. Maybe it was all he'd known since he was a young man, the feeling that he didn't know where he'd be staying on a given night, or who with.

Whatever problems he was having off the table, he was still playing good snooker. So good, in fact, that his performance at Sheffield in 1994 still ranks as his best chance to lift the title. He won his first round match 10-6 against the Scot Billy Snaddon. Next up was Neal Foulds. This was a tough test. He eventually fell over the line at 13-10 before beating a young Ken Doherty by the same scoreline in the next round. Things looked like they were getting harder and harder, but the semi-final was something of an anti-climax as he comfortably disposed of Darren Morgan 16-8.

In the final he faced who else but Stephen Hendry, Jimmy's new nemesis. In the first round Hendry had played Surrinda Gill, hardly a household name. He nearly knocked in a maximum in this match, potting 15 reds and colours before failing on a long yellow.

Just before his second round match against Dave Harold that year Hendry slipped in his hotel bathroom and fractured his left arm. Harold must have fancied his chances at this point, but after getting a pain-killing injection Hendry devoured him 13-2. It was an incredible demolition job, made all the more baffling considering his arm was so weak he couldn't even lift the rest, having to get the referee to do it for him. Once that hurdle was negotiated maybe it wasn't surprising that he dispatched everyone else in his way.

So Jimmy had drawn the short straw again. It was almost becoming a joke, what one journalist dubbed 'The Annual Jimmy White Screw-Up Competition' (and he wasn't talking about a type of shot). Would we witness another lamb to the slaughter scenario? Or would there be a twist in the White-Hendry tale?

By now one might have felt that they could call the Crucible 'the White house'. Jimmy had made it his home from home, always pulling something extra out for this venue even after sluggish seasons in front of a crowd utterly dedicated to him.

He got off to his by now familiar bad start in the final, trailing 5-1, but amazingly led 9-7 after the first day's play. Was this the year?

It was nip and tuck the following day, but eventually the score stood at 16-16, and then 17-17. I wasn't sure if my heart could stand many more of these knife-edge thrillers. It was down to the final frame again.

In the decider Jimmy led by 37 points to 28 and was playing a black off its spot. It wasn't a difficult pot, but when you're perhaps five minutes away from being a world champion anything is difficult, especially if your name is Jimmy White.

You could almost feel Jimmy hyperventilating. You could almost hear him saying to himself, 'This is my one, son'. Most players would have slowed down or stopped to take a sip of water, but that was never Jimmy's way. He was a rebel without a pause.

He missed the black and a gasp went round the auditorium. He'd undercut it hugely. Worse still, he left it in the open. And, because he was in the middle of a break, there were also reds available.

It was time to panic, and I did. I had been kneeling on the floor uttering incantations to the television as per usual and when the black missed the pocket I jumped up and lashed my clenched fist into a lampshade that was sitting on top of the set, sending it hurtling to the floor. For a moment I didn't feel any pain. The shock had numbed it. I was still watching the screen, watching Hendry come to the table. It was only as he started potting balls that I noticed my hand swelling up. There was no blood, but I ran to the kitchen for a basin and filled it with cold water, dunking my hand into it and then picking it up and rushing back to the TV. Hendry was still at the table. The pain sang through my veins – and my heart. In one way it was good for me. My throbbing hand distracted me from what was happening in Sheffield – the beginning of the end. Of a match and possibly a career.

By now my left hand, which I used for punching as well as snooker, had swollen up to twice the size of my right one. It was almost comical to behold. To my disbelieving eyes it looked as if it was even bigger in the basin, as if it was shivering under the water. On the television Jimmy was talking to David Vine. I hadn't even registered Hendry's moment of triumph. I had seen it and not seen it. It was like a scene glimpsed from memory.

"He's beginning to annoy me," said Jimmy, smiling. Once again he was Jimmy the Gent. *The young bairn is beginning to annoy more than you, mate*, I thought.

Another loser's medal to add to his ever-growing collection, while Hendry got the booty. Five runners-up prizes in a row at the Crucible. How anyone could cope with such disappointment I just couldn't fathom.

As for myself, the pain in my hand worsened. It was as if there was a creature inside my fist. I knew I had to have it seen to somewhere, but I didn't really have the spirit to get myself to hospital. I had nothing left in me. Jimmy had sucked it all out.

Somehow I summoned up the gumption to drive to the nearest hospital, which isn't easy when you're trying to change gear with a dead hand. I parked the car and walked into the Casualty area where a number of people sat, some of them with crutches and bandages. When the nurse on duty saw my hand she said, "Jesus! What happened to you?"

I could hardly say 'Jimmy White missed the black' as she'd probably have referred me to the psychiatric unit.

"I injured my hand," I muttered under my breath, stating the bleeding obvious. She dressed the wound and gave me some pills to take. She wrote out a prescription and I sat under observation for a while. I'm not sure how long. Time was hazy, as was everything else.

I drove all the way home in second gear: it was too much agony to change gears. When I got back to the house the television was still on. The snooker was over, obviously, so I sat watching a gardening programme in a daze. As I ran through my mind the events that vaguely seemed to have happened not hours but days ago I felt like I wanted to throw up.

I started thinking about why Jimmy had missed the pot and came up with three possible reasons. The first, needless to say, was pressure. He'd been fighting a rearguard action through most of the match and had hardly relaxed since it began. He hadn't gone on one of his rolls, aside from the one which had brought him back into the match on the first day. Secondly, the pressure was increased because he wasn't in a big lead and every ball was like a match ball. If he missed, he knew Hendry could clear up. Thirdly, he had his eyes on 'the prize' rather than the table.

So therefore he threw his cue at that black. The rest is history.

There's a fourth possibility, as Clive Everton pointed out in his commentary. Jimmy's rhythm had been broken by a previous shot where he'd spent a long time putting the extension on the long rest and then taking it off again after changing his mind. Could that have cost him the opportunity of finally winning the World title in his sixth final?

Maybe it was a combination of all of these factors.

After a 13-year pilgrimage to Sheffield it was the supreme agony to be so near and yet so far. But snooker is a game in which millimetres separate winners from losers. Every player walks this gangplank and Jimmy much more than most. After he missed the black by the proverbial mile he probably knew the game was up – in all senses. With a look of resignation, he slumped back into his chair as Hendry stepped in for the kill.

As Jimmy had looked poised to win his first world title, Hendry later admitted, "I was delighted for him when he got in. Anyone else and I would have hated it. I was ready to shake his hand." A few minutes later he did, but as victim rather than conqueror. So Hendry hadn't even wanted the chance, or at least not as badly as he would have against another player, or if he hadn't already had so many world titles under his belt. But he had too much respect for Jimmy not to take the opportunity when it came to him. So he twisted the knife into his friend for the sixth time.

Jimmy's own explanation was simply, "I twitched. I was afraid to miss, so I missed. It happens as you get older. When you start playing you can't wait to get to the table, but when you've lost key matches you're too aware of the dangers, too afraid, because you're playing on your memory."

He also said, which seems contradictory, "I took it for granted. Instead of thinking of the game I was working on my victory speech in my head. I'll thank him ... must remember to thank her ... I won't thank him. I felt like an Oscar winner in that final frame. But it's never over till it's over."

One can understand a Hendry or a Davis feeling that confident, having bagged world trophies before, but how could Jimmy? Especially when Hendry only needed one frame, and when he'd punished Jimmy so often in the past? I felt Jimmy was a bit like failed pugilist Terry Malloy, the character played by Marlon Brando in the classic film *On the Waterfront*. Brando said he was never asked about any part as much as this, because most people were losers in life and they could identify so much with his line, "I coulda bin a contender, Charlie."

In his book *Frame and Fortune* Steve Davis wrote, 'Jimmy misses like that because he plays every shot at the same pace. The trouble is, he never takes into account the state of the game. Some shots require a more sedate approach. They might not be more difficult in potting terms, but the state of the game might require more caution.' Jimmy, Davis believed, didn't bother with context: 'He always wants to get on with the show', with the result that he left himself 'no time to breathe'.

I was, of course, desperate for Jimmy to win this match, but in a strange kind of way a tiny part of my subconscious didn't want him to. I was scared that if he won he might retire and that would have been catastrophic. What would I do without Jimmy? I wanted him to play until he was 90. Winning this match, I felt, would have given him an excuse to ride off into the Sheffield sunset and party like there was no tomorrow. It was, as it happened, his 32nd birthday. But I doubt if he blew out many candles that night.

Jimmy once confessed that his mother worried about him winning a World title early on in his career for fear of what it would do to him. Maybe she shared my concerns that he'd hit the bottle harder once the mountain was climbed. But by 1994 she felt he could handle it. When he failed to pot that black and a few minutes later shook a world champion's hand for the fifth time in as many years as a runner-up, she cried. As many of his fans did. And perhaps Jimmy too. There comes a time in the affairs of men which, taken at the flood, leads on to better things. But this was a cruel way to lose and I felt that Jimmy would have a hard time recovering from it.

Six World finals and six defeats. So what now – come back next year for more of the same? More immediately, Jimmy needed to lick his wounds. Would he drown his sorrows in the nearest tavern? Play cards with Higgins?

I recalled what Charlie Sheen said in the movie *Platoon*: "I think now, looking back, we didn't fight the enemy, we fought ourselves. The enemy was in us. The war is over for me now, but it will always be there, the rest of my days." Could Jimmy come back from this? Could anyone? The scoreline and the manner of defeat would have brutalised the soul of any player, and I knew Jimmy was more fragile than most. The difference was, he didn't show it. He internalised it, and that made the potential reaction all the worse when he got back to his dressing room. I once read that Hendry threw a cue across his dressing room once after a defeat. Jimmy was different. He just smiled sadly. But inside him there must have been a Mount Etna waiting to erupt.

Afterwards he said he had angry people sending him letters with betting slips enclosed, saying things like, 'Our family can't go on holiday because we were going to win this amount of money on you.' Each and every such piece of correspondence killed him. I remembered John McCririck saying, "If Jimmy White was a horse, the bookies would feed him free oats for the rest of his life." But my money had gone on Hendry that day. I needed some solace if/when Jimmy lost.

Other letters he received were more friendly. There was even one from a granny which said, 'Come and stay with me for a week and get over your loss.' That touched him.

A part of me felt that Jimmy had spent so long chasing his dream he'd almost forgotten what he was chasing any more. Or maybe he liked the chase more than its realisation. There's a scene in Evan Hunter's book *Strangers When We Meet* where a writer who's been struggling finally attains critical success, but feels himself underwhelmed by it. '"Why shouldn't I be deliriously happy right now?" he asks his friend, "What do I do if I win the Nobel Prize someday? Put a bullet in my head?"'

He goes on to say that are two American 'carrots': 'The man-carrot is Success and the woman-carrot is Beauty.' But carrots, he adds, 'are for rabbits'.

Paul Newman, Jimmy's hero from *The Hustler*, said something similar after he finally won an Oscar after being nominated six times. "A long time ago," he told *Photoplay* magazine, "winning was very important, but it's like chasing a beautiful woman. You hang in there for years. Then she finally relents and you say, 'Honey, I'm too tired.'" Was Jimmy too tired now? Was this another reason he possibly missed the black? Because it was too available? Maybe some Freudian analyst will come along in the next generation with such a theory. For now, though, all that mattered was that the fish was off the hook. Once again it had slipped downstream to swim with all the sharks.

It was also a bit like the last scene in the film *The Cincinnati Kid* in which Steve McQueen is beaten by The Man (Edward G. Robinson), and ends up playing a child's coin game with a black child, even losing that. "You're jes' not good enough for me yet," the black kid says in that film's final frame, speaking to McQueen and maybe even Jimmy White.

Because I now realised that The Man would always be there waiting for him, either in the guise of Reardon, Davis, Hendry or whatever new Hendry the future threw up. Jimmy would take his punishment the way he always took it, slowly and painfully, having learned nothing at all from defeat, and thus consigned to more and more humblings at the same hands until one day he either hung up his cue in frustration or decided to transmogrify his personality completely.

After leaving Sheffield, Jimmy took his wrath out on the house he was living in: "I was serving a three-year ban for drink driving at the time, so I couldn't really go anywhere. I got heavily into DIY, but proceeded to do more damage than good. I wrecked the place really." In the process he probably got a lot of tension out of himself, although I couldn't help thinking that he should have just bought himself a dartboard with Hendry's face on it and have done with it.

His results for the 1994/95 season seemed reflective of Jimmy's poor state of mind. He went out 5-1 to Nigel Bond in the second round of the Dubai Classic. The Scottish player Euan Henderson, who failed to make any impact on snooker, beat him 5-2 at the same stage of the Grand Prix. In the second round of the UK he was annihilated 9-3 by Jason Ferguson. A veritably unknown player called Mick Price beat him twice, 5-4 in the second round of the Welsh Open and 5-2 in the third round of the British Open.

He did reach the semi-final of the International tournament only to be denied by his old adversary Steve Davis 6-4. In the first round of the Thailand Open Mark Johnston-Allen beat him 5- 2. That left the World Championship. Surely it wouldn't be another White-Hendry duel. In fact it couldn't because they were seeded to meet in the semis, which they did, but Hendry prevailed 16-12. That victory included a maximum break ... by Stephen Hendry. Not Jimmy White. In the Dr Martens league Jimmy slumped to a 6-1 defeat at the hands of Hendry to complete his misery.

Hendry has been called the greatest player ever to lift a cue, but such superlatives have also been showered on the likes of Joe and Steve Davis, Ronnie O'Sullivan and even Jimmy. In factual terms Hendry holds the lead in world titles in the modern game (7) as well as career centuries (over 700). He's a brave player and an exciting one, but also somebody with an inbuilt sense of when to pounce, like a jockey coming up on the blind side to win. He has the best of Davis and also a smattering of White. At his peak he was unplayable, as his record attests to. Jimmy White's misfortune was that the two greatest players in the modern game were at the peak of their powers throughout the entire course of his career.

In an interview with Jon Wilde of *Loaded* magazine, Jimmy admitted what would happen if he failed to win the World Championship. He said, "In that case

I'll end up as some sad old fucker who sits around talking about the ones that got away."

* * *

Towards the end of 1994 a video came out called *Close to the Wind* which was a kind of mini-biography of Jimmy. He had just appeared in his sixth World final and lost it by a whisker. Did somebody feel this was it for him on the big stage? If so they were very prescient.

The timing of the video may have been ominous, but Jimmy, as ever, was upbeat. In it he told us he would win the World title not once but a few times. (But he didn't want to sound "greedy".)

His parents were interviewed, sipping drinks in a leafy setting and reminiscing about him as a child. Tommy spoke of him as if he was his golden boy but Lil, his mother, said he could be a little devil when he wanted.

The video also brought us inside Zan's snooker hall, where Jimmy had honed his trade. He said he first entered it simply to get in out of the rain with his friends. One of them had a few quid, so they began bashing balls about. He was soon bitten by the bug. It was that simple.

In a sense the video demythologised the Jimmy White story for me. Zan's, which was also pictured from the outside, didn't look at all magical. It looked just like any other inner-city snooker hall. It also looked too organised, but maybe it had been different two decades before when Jimmy first became entranced by it.

The manager himself, Ted Zanicelli, was also interviewed. He told us Jimmy was so good he eventually had to ban him from playing money matches.

Arthur Beatty, his kindly former teacher who had allowed Jimmy a measured amount of truancy, also appeared. "I told him there was no money in snooker," he admitted. It showed how much teachers knew about life. "How is Mr Beatty?" Jimmy excitedly asked his interviewer when his name came up. You could see his respect for him was huge. Calling him 'Mr' many years after leaving the school sounded funny, especially when the progressive teacher didn't look too much older than Jimmy.

Jimmy admitted he regretted not spending more time in school. "If I wrote you a letter," he told his interviewer, "there would be some mistakes in it." Although to me this seemed a small price to pay for being a millionaire.

There were tributes from the players who beat him at Sheffield in world finals – Davis, Parrott and Hendry. Davis recalled meeting him for the first time at Ron Gross's snooker hall in Neasdon when Jimmy was playing snooker with a walking stick, having broken his leg. "I'm sure he made a century with it," the

Nugget trilled, acknowledging that Jimmy was already a legend with his friends who seemed to know he would be mega in the game even at 15.

Jimmy said he should have gone pro after winning the World Amateur title. For some reason he didn't consider it feasible at the time. It would have given him two more years at Sheffield. (I thought, *that would have given him two more years in which to lose two more finals?*)

Win or lose, though, it was clear that his mother regarded him as a world champion even as a runner-up. "We have a party even when he loses," she chirped. *Maybe*, I thought, *this was part of the problem*. It was almost as if the distinction between success and failure was non-existent for her.

His dad was different. Anytime Jimmy lost a big match Tommy went to bed early to lick his wounds – because he knew how much it meant to Jimmy.

John Parrott was very complimentary about him, as was Hendry. Tony Meo, for some reason, didn't appear. It would have been interesting to hear his childhood memories of his buddy. It would also have been nice to hear from Jimmy's brothers, but they all seem to be media-shy.

Jimmy's daughter Lauren was pictured standing behind her dad at one point, looking remarkably like him. She seemed slightly awed by him as he spoke about what snooker had done for him. The money, he said, wasn't as important as the places he got to see and the people he'd met. I wondered how much Lauren had known about his wild escapades. ("I kept my children away from that side of my life," he said in another interview, "but if they Googled me today they'd probably get some of it".)

Alex Higgins was predictably forthcoming about him, calling him "mercurial", the term that had so often been applied to himself. He talked about the classic semi-final of 1982 as being a seminal point in Jimmy's career. That failure seemed to define him somehow. Jimmy was gracious enough to admit that even if he'd won it, Reardon (who was waiting for the winner in the final) might have had the safety game to turn him over. (This attitude was in marked contrast to anything Jimmy had said to me over the years, when his chutzpah was in overload.) Higgins's overall summation of him was that he "tried too hard".

Jimmy also admitted he was "silly" about many aspects of his life and career. "Don't they say there's a thin line between genius and cranky," he opined, putting on one of his funny faces when he said the word "cranky". I think he meant there was a thin line between genius and madness, but this was Jimmy after all, a man with his own vocabulary (maybe he wasn't at school the day Mr Beatty gave his madness lesson.)

All the seminal moments of his career were in the video, including the brilliant 147 he made in Sheffield in 1992. We also got parts of Kirk Stevens's maximum in the 1984 Benson & Hedges Masters which he made against Jimmy, although Jimmy, of course, won that match. In the following frame he produced two sensational shots to end it. The first was a shot from pink to black where he screwed the cue ball the length of the table in a manner that seemed to defy the laws of geometry, landing perfectly on the black with a gallon of reverse side. His banana shot on the black, also with reverse side, was equally scintillating. "I don't play those ones too much any more," he admitted in the video, "they wear out the tip of the cue." Pity.

The video was a tremendous reminder of his snooker genius and a fascinating account of his life even if, like most documentaries dealing with this man, it failed to address the deeper reasons behind why he failed to negotiate what Davis called "the final hurdle" at Sheffield. As Oscar Wilde once said, "To lose one child may be regarded as an accident, but to lose two has to be put down to negligence." What would Oscar have said about losing six?

At the end of the video Jimmy said he was going to retire in 2004, but he sounded about as convincing as Frank Sinatra on a similar theme. *Thank God*, I thought. *What would I have done without him?*

THE ENEMY

AS THE YEARS went on and Jimmy's title chances started to dwindle due to his increasingly kamikaze style of play, which saw any thought of safety laughed off in favour of a long pot, and then another one, it looked like his sell-by date could be imminent. I took notes at most of these matches and kept the videos, dreaming about the day I could show them all to him and point out his mistakes to him. Every time he lost, some commentator like Clive Everton would say something like "Form is temporary, but class is permanent", the cliché that let Jimmy off the hook. I felt more urgency than this was needed to halt his slide.

"Is Jimmy *still* getting mugged by idiots?" Hugo continued to say to me, but I told him I didn't follow him either because he won or lost; I followed him because I loved the way he played the game. "He's his own worst enemy," he said, but I felt that was beside the point ... that if Jimmy lost a game it was usually because he was trying to do too much.

"You'd imagine he'd have wised up to his problems by now," was another familiar taunt. I agreed with this, but I also knew that if he got too wise he mightn't be Jimmy anymore. So maybe losing was the price to be paid for the thrills he gave me.

Whenever Jimmy won a match, of course, all the fair weather friends came out of the woodwork and went, "Good on you, my son, I always knew you had it in you."

Journalist Jean Rafferty calls snooker 'the cruel game'. This it certainly is. In most other contests between two people they slug it out together, but in snooker only one man plays at a time, which means that if you screw up there's generally little you can do about it. Sitting in your seat as your opponent mops up is the loneliest experience in the world. It's also one of the most frustrating ones. I had to sit in that seat a thousand times alongside Jimmy.

"Ditch him," people would say to me, "he's not worth it. You're putting yourself through the pain barrier again, and for what? Sport is supposed to be a leisure pursuit, something you watch with your feet up after doing your 40 hours on the job."

People from the club I played in told me he was history whenever he got beaten by a lesser player. That was it for them. No nuances, no fancy extrapolations. Jimmy was fucked. End of story. Another past star on snooker's tip, another classic victim of premature burn-out.

They couldn't appreciate anything beyond this empirical database. The stark facts. Jimmy was no longer winning, sure, but I'd go home and watch a video of the match and see a hundred different reasons why he lost. It might have been a shout from the crowd, a piece of dust on the table, an unkind run of the ball. I knew Jimmy was such a cerebral kind of player, anything was capable of wrecking his nervous system. Deep down I knew he still had it in him physically, but because I was too devastated to argue I'd go along with what they said. I was as mentally shot as Jimmy. Yeah, Jimmy was fucked. Yesterday's Man. Another Higgins.

What amazed me about these people was their coldness. I had a romantic attitude to the game, but they were dismissing a genius as an also-ran. I could never get my head around that kind of arrogant thinking. When I met Jimmy I saw him as a dreamy child in comparison to these slick wannabes who knew the price of everything and the value of nothing. Their cynicism made me sick.

In the years after the classic 1994 World final between Jimmy and Hendry, the main question in snooker circles was, 'Who's going to beat Jimmy White in the World final this year?' It was cruel but understandable. On the other hand I liked Neal Fould's comment when he was asked if he sympathised with Jimmy for his incomplete Sheffield record. "If that's incomplete," Foulds emoted, "I wish I could be incomplete."

I took his point. Okay, so Jimmy lost six world finals but there are hundreds of players out there who've never even been in one, or close to it. When we look at it from this point of view, failure becomes a very relative term indeed.

As well as the six Sheffield finals Jimmy also reached four semi-finals and five quarter-finals. That's 15 quarter-finals between 1980 and 2000, an incredible feat.

Every time he lost there seemed to be a surge of disappointment round Britain, if not the world. I always went into a decline myself, perhaps even a bigger one than Jimmy, and couldn't bring myself to watch the remainder of tournaments he was no longer a part of. It was like Hamlet without the Prince. This was the kind of presence Jimmy had. You needed to be on the edge of your seat watching him walk that tightrope as he dragged on a cigarette before building himself up to one of those mad shots that won or lost him frames.

Was this out of proportion? A reporter said to the author Mordecai Richler one day at Goffs after Jimmy had been beaten, "Everybody feels sorry for fucking Jimmy White, but he owns property worth more than a million quid in London." But surely this was to miss the point. It wasn't about money. This was show business. Or soap opera. You felt for (and with) his vulnerable soul. You knew how much it meant to him and therefore it meant that much to you too.

Some people shared Richler's sardonic attitude. Julie Welch wrote, 'The game has lost its sleaze and is all the poorer for that. Snooker was exciting when it was raw and new and the halls were a haven for boys skipping school. Jimmy White was sixteen and lived in a council house in Tooting with a broken bell. Now he's as respectable as a bishop.'

I also came across the same kind of attitudes when I was trying to interview Jimmy, when I had to go through the PR people and all the red tape. I found a lot of these people to be heartless and self-serving. They also had big heads. And then when I met Jimmy he was the complete opposite. He had no airs and graces. The nobodies protecting him were The Enemy. It was a classic irony.

The same was true of his attitude to the game. He wouldn't remember scores or dates like the people round him. He mightn't even know technical details. His buccaneering spirit just wanted to pot balls. He wasn't in it for money like the people handling him. It wasn't a job, it was a vocation, a way of life. Jimmy played match finals with the same attitude he did a Tuesday morning knock-up in the local fleapit. You either loved snooker or you didn't.

I loved him all the more for that.

For Jimmy, glory wasn't what it was about. What it was about was trying to perfect your style, to do the right thing, to not choke or chicken out or go for the easy option. No, Jimmy would always have to crowd please, even if it killed him. And more often than not it did.

Sometimes he played such wild shots I found myself almost hoping he'd lose. I told myself if he gets the lard kicked out of him often enough by gobdaws it might give him the shot in the arm he needed to realise his game was in crisis. What I hated about him was that no matter how often he lost to no-hopers in dead-end venues he always came into the next tournament full of confidence about going 'all the way' But then that was what I loved about him too.

As I listened to him deliver this kind of bull to some slavering mike-man, I'd think, *Jimmy, it might be worth thinking about winning your first match against the World's number 122 before you book your place in the final* ... because I'd seen him perish at that particular juncture more than once in the past. I knew he needed to develop a harder edge, to put his opponents under the cosh, to act the bad ass – like Davis.

I sometimes put these thoughts in print in newspaper articles and got a fusillade of abuse from people who said that Steve Davis was a perfect gentleman and where did I get off with this kind of gratuitous abuse. I even got some hate mail directed to my house. Davis, I learned, had a lot of friends. These were usually composed of the type of people who regarded Jimmy White as being too flash, too egoistic, too show-offy. As we play, so do we think, and many anally-retentive people were as irked by Jimmy's unpredictability as I was by Davis's compart-mentalised mind.

When Jimmy joined Barry Hearn's Matchroom team I felt it was like some supreme form of treachery to me. Matchroom was where Davis was. For me it was like Billy the Kid selling out to Pat Garret. They'd had this decade-long rivalry and now they were to be stablemates. I couldn't quite figure this out and it made it hard for me to approach their subsequent tussles with the same degree of enthusiasm, as I said to Jimmy.

Some other people disliked Davis's style as much as I did. I remember once when he was playing in Goffs and a writer who was no great lover of him said he hoped he won his first match. The reason was a bit obscure: he would be playing Higgins in the next round, and this would mean the Belfastman could then "nail the bastard".

Before many of his matches Jimmy would be favourite and lose. Pitted against the same player soon after, he would be favourite again and again lose. If he lost a third time he'd still be short-priced and I'd think, what does he have to do to become a 2/1 shot in a two horse race – cut off one of his hands? Develop a wasting disease? Start playing with a bamboo cane? Then I remembered the story of him making a century with a walking stick and realised even that wouldn't have made any difference.

The reality was that the bookies knew that Jimmy lovers like me would shell out hard cash to support our man, even though we knew he was ultimately doomed to failure. But for a while I started to bet against him. My thinking was that if/when he lost at least I'd have a few bob to quell my depression. But then there were occasions when his brilliance made me think he should be favourite for every match he played. I remember one such night in Goffs when he seemed dead and buried, but still managed to compose himself for a last burst to win the match in dramatic fashion. This was, as Jack Nicholson might say, as good as it gets.

I was on the sauce that night (a not unprecedented phenomenon) and found myself lying down on the main floor of the foyer screaming in jubilation as the crowds flooded out around me. This was what Jimmy White could still do to me.

Another night when Jimmy won from being two down with three to play I got so excited I stood outside the car park not letting people go home. I wanted them all to stay and celebrate. One driver, after giving me the Harvey Smith Vs, shouted out his window, "What are you on?"

It was just beer ... and the elation of victory that made me drunk. And really, it wasn't the alcohol.

Then the driver, irked that I wouldn't give way, proceeded to run over my foot as he forced his way out. I didn't feel the pain until the next morning.

COVER UP

1995 WAS JIMMY'S *annus horribilis*. First of all his brother Martin was diagnosed with cancer. Then the Inland Revenue declared Jimmy bankrupt with debts of more than £170,000. Not surprisingly, he felt like throwing in the towel completely. He lost 11 matches on the spin and fell into a deep depression.

In January of that year he appeared in an ad for Cover Up, a cosmetic that replaced bald spots by enhancing the tiny hairs on one's head. Jimmy had a bald spot that had become very noticeable in aerial camera shots during matches. To try and cure this he underwent an operation that involved the insertion of a piece of plastic under his scalp. But it went wrong and he suffered much swelling and pain. It was so bad he had to withdraw from the European Open that year.

He went into a different kind of operating room after he visited his GP for a routine check-up for insurance purposes and casually mentioned that he had "a bit of a lump" on his left testicle. "If it had been a woman doctor," Jimmy told Graham Bridgstock of the *Daily Mail*, "I might not have said anything about it at all."

The GP said he didn't like the look of it and sent him to a clinic. The next day a surgeon examined him and said, "Don't have anything to eat for 12 hours. I'll see you tomorrow after the operation." Jimmy couldn't believe what he was hearing and immediately went into panic mode, thinking, *I have a wife and young children. I don't want to die.*

He wasn't going to tell Maureen, but in the end Jimmy decided he would in case he didn't survive the surgery. During the operation two malignant growths were discovered and removed. He spent a few days in bed and a week later he was playing snooker again.

"No-one really knows what caused it," Jimmy told Bridgstock. "It could have been stress-related." He promised to have himself tested every three months to make sure it didn't recur.

The operation for testicular cancer had been in March 1995. His son Tommy Tiger, who was born three years later, became living proof that you can not only survive with one testicle but that everything can still be in working order.

Jimmy told Bridgstock, "Over the years I've been in a lot of trouble, but I've always managed to switch off and play. To be honest, most of my troubles – bankruptcy, drinking, gambling – were self-inflicted. But cancer is one thing I can't blame myself for. I am just a very, very lucky guy to have caught it in time. Either way, it's worked wonders for me. In the past I'd lose and not talk for a few days. I'd become strange. Difficult to live with. Now I'm totally different. I've a new perspective on life and I'm less stressed. I'm mellower, really relaxed. It takes a lot to upset me. Some people take the view that I'm too laid back. Yet it's how I feel. OK, snooker is important to me because it's my career. But after cancer it's only a game."

His brother Martin wasn't so lucky. He died from his cancer. Jimmy was devastated by this and also by the fact that another one of his brothers, Tommy, was fighting lymphoma.

Jimmy and his family decided to 'wake' Martin after he died. They were toasting his memory when someone said, "Let's get Martin from the morgue. He should be here."

They went to the morgue, talked their way in, lifted Martin out of his coffin and took him home. Jimmy said, "I walked him out in his best suit. The driver of the car I was in assumed he was just another drunk. Back home we sat him in the chair of honour, put a drink in front of him and dealt him a hand of cards. It was a good party and we all felt better afterwards."

When they got him into the taxi for the drive back to the morgue the driver said, "He doesn't look too well, Jimmy," which was probably the biggest understatement since Noah said it looked like rain.

Things were so bad for Jimmy at this point he needed a touch of absurdity to keep himself sane, which presented itself when Tony Meo revealed that he too had contracted testicular cancer. When Jimmy heard this he joked, "It must have been something we picked up in the back of Dodgy Bob's taxi!"

Having to deal with his bankruptcy took his mind off health concerns. Jimmy confessed that he'd blown over £3 million on drink, gambling and high living. But that didn't shock anyone who'd followed his life closely. The only surprise in fact was that he could work out how much he'd spent.

Things were almost as dramatic on the table, although for other reasons. He'd been playing in the first round of the 1993 World Championships and leading 7-2, when he was informed that an enormous amount of money had been placed in various bookies' offices around the West End and elsewhere on a 10-2 scoreline. Undeterred, he went on to play his best and did indeed defeat his opponent Peter Francisco by that margin. The match was investigated by police afterwards but Jimmy was cleared of any wrongdoing. Francisco wasn't so fortunate, effectively being turfed out of the game for suspected involvement in the betting sting.

Peter's uncle, Silvino, had also been involved in match-fixing allegations, the most notable being his 5-1 defeat to Terry Griffiths in the 1989 Benson & Hedges Masters. Also under suspicion were a defeat to Tony Knowles in the same event three years previously, and a victory over Peter in the 1987 Mercantile Credit Classic, the latter two matches also having this scoreline.

Steve Davis suspected Francisco of throwing a match against him in Plymouth in 1994, so much so that he even gifted him a frame in what turned out to be yet another 5-1 defeat of the South African. In that instance, many bets had been placed on Francisco to lose by either 5-0 or 5-1.

If Francisco was intending to lose this match against Jimmy 10-2, and anyone who's seen the video would probably agree he was, he didn't do himself any favours by winning the fourth frame (in which he needed a snooker) to square things at 2-2 going into the first interval. By the law of probability, one's luck evens out over long matches so even if Francisco wasn't playing to par and Jimmy was flying, there was every chance he'd get a frame-winning opportunity from being 3-1 down. When one is throwing a match this isn't good thinking as it increases the chances of being caught. To lose eight frames on the spin as Francisco did, and to lose them to a man not playing out of his skin, was asking a lot. In the commentary box Dennis Taylor and Clive Everton were left scratching their heads in every other frame over Francisco's amateurish antics.

It's very difficult to prove conclusively that anybody intentionally lost a match, but the decisions of the WPBSA on these matters, arrived at by a combination of background research and considered viewing of the matches in question by seasoned professionals, have never been questioned.

Snooker would continue to be dogged by match-fixing rumours and counter-rumours in the following years as irregular betting habits raised suspicions of coups. Quinten Hann was suspended from the game for eight years in 2006 as a result of a sting operation by the *Sun* newspaper. Hann was suspected of throwing a match against the Scot Marcus Campbell, of trying to persuade his fellow Aussie

Neil Robertson to throw another one, and of considering being whitewashed by Ken Doherty in a third. More recently, Jamie Burnett fell under suspicion of deliberately losing to Stephen Maguire.

Other sports have suffered from such distasteful practices too; racing, football and cricket being high profile cases in point.

Jimmy freely admits he was offered money to throw matches in the past, but didn't succumb. It's hard to imagine anyone who could be less tempted, so great is his will to win. Maybe that's why Francisco thought he was onto a good thing. But nobody should expect Jimmy to beat them 10-2, even when he was in his prime. All too often he had a bad day at the office, particularly when he'd been on the tiles the night before – which was too often for his own good.

* * *

Jimmy lost his mother in 1996. Lily was one of the mainstays of his life, a woman he seldom spoke of but loved dearly. She kept in the background mostly, but she cared deeply for her hugely gifted son and always wanted the best for him. No more than any mother who never thinks any of her children will become famous, Lily had to adjust to the attention Jimmy brought on himself and the attendant media pressures. She feared he'd become carried away with success in his 20s, but once Jimmy became a British institution she relaxed and enjoyed herself.

Coming on the back of Martin's death, Jimmy's grief was doubled. It was almost as if the deaths were an outreach from his failure to deliver the World trophy to them. Like the rest of us, Martin and Lily had cheered and hoped to every last Sheffield ball. Sadly, they had nothing to show for it at the end but memories.

Britain loved Jimmy but you couldn't put love on your cabinet or raise it aloft on your shoulders. I knew how closely-knit Jimmy's family was, and how inconsolable their emotions were at this time, having got to know his father fairly well over the years. I knew how old-world his affections were and how he refused to big them up. He was as taciturn about his family as he was about his life and his game. Most people in snooker regarded Jimmy as an unknown quantity, an incorrigible rascal. He drew the line at inviting people into his heart. Being loved by the public might have meant you had to sign an autograph, but it didn't give them provenance into your inner life.

Dennis Taylor had won the 1984 Rothman's Grand Prix shortly after his mother died. Her passing, he believed, gave him the iron in the soul he needed to compete properly in the white-hot pressures of snooker. It was his first major title after being a struggler on the circuit since he went professional. It led on to his incredible 1985 World title triumph over Davis.

Taylor annihilated Cliff Thorburn 10-2 in this final, just three weeks after his mother passed away. Granted Thorburn had done him a favour by knocking Davis out in the semi-finals (and was probably burned out somewhat after the effort of that match) but it was still a massive achievement for the journeyman pro.

Jimmy's game, in contrast, fell apart after his mother died. Maybe it was getting ready to anyway, after his cancer scare and Martin's death. But tragedy can affect different players in different ways. Ronnie O'Sullivan said he became more focussed when his father was sentenced to 18 years in prison for murder. In this he was like Taylor. Jimmy evinced a more normal reaction to an off-the-table tragedy; he crumbled.

Steve Davis likes to say, "You have to play snooker like it means nothing when it means everything." Jimmy couldn't quite do that. In the aftermath of Lily's death he wore his heart even more on his sleeve and started to go for even more impossible shots. Sometimes he looked like he couldn't wait to be out of the playing area. He needed to hide in the dressing room, in the pub, at the track. Maybe he even needed to hide from himself. His hand was pushing the cue forward, but his mind was out to lunch. The upshot was that he plummeted down the rankings like a ski-jumper falling out of the sky. A casual observer could have been forgiven for thinking they were watching a nervous breakdown in slow motion. The lights were on but there was nobody home. The whirlwind had become a gentle zephyr.

Two other events happened to Jimmy in 1996. He was convicted of drunk driving and also had his dog Splinter kidnapped (he paid £300 for the canine's return.) He was having more problems with Maureen too at this point of his life and they were reflected in his poor form at the table. He slumped to defeat after defeat, finding it difficult to practise or concentrate. Watching him you felt you were seeing a man on the edge. Every time he came to the table he seemed to be creating problems that weren't there. Clearances that had once seemed so simple were now problematic. His safety play was still sloppy and his shot selection baffling. It's okay to go for everything when you're on top form, but when you're struggling you have to be more conservative. Jimmy wasn't.

He played as he always had, in the crash-bang style, and gifted opportunities to his opponents. Sometimes I felt he could have been beaten by a middling club player in these matches. Even when he went ahead you felt he was going to be caught. He looked edgy and uncomfortable, as if he was almost looking forward to being dead in the water.

Joe Swail beat him in the second round of the Thailand Classic. He lost to John Higgins in the quarter-finals of the Grand Prix. Higgins also eliminated him from the UK Championship in the third round. He went out to Steve James in the first round of the German Open and to Chris Small by the odd frame in the second round of the Welsh. He was trounced by Dave Finbow in the first round of the International and beaten 5-2 by Steve James in the first round of the European Open. Fergal O'Brien beat him 5-3 in the second round of the British Open and Peter Ebdon took him out by the same margin in the Thailand Open.

It was carnage, which reached its zenith in the 1996 Masters quarter-final when he was up against Hendry, who thrashed him 6-0. This victory included three century breaks and, at one point of the match, a humiliating tally of 487 unanswered points. Just as Davis had caned him repeatedly in the 80s, the relentless Scot was doling out the same medicine in this decade, and not only at the Crucible.

From a situation like this it's hard to imagine anyone coming back. In other sports you can put a bad shot to the back of your mind as you're straight back into the fray, but in snooker you often sit in your chair to see your opponent clear the table from it. The atmosphere is quiet and claustrophobic. Team games like soccer permit you to interact or to work off tensions by running around a pitch. In snooker one sits in a corner and broods over missed chances. When you eventually get back to the table – not soon, usually, if it's Hendry you're playing – it's difficult to work up a rhythm again.

The following year Jimmy emerged from this career low when he played Peter Ebdon in the second round of the World Championships at Sheffield. If the drama of 1994 had been high, this equalled it. It was a best of 25 frame match and each player was up for it.

Ebdon, the son of a prison officer, was keeping Jimmy in jail for prolonged periods of the match. That prevented him getting much rhythm going. Some opponents fell into Jimmy's pace and paid the price, but now, as his consistency faltered, a new generation of players who'd watched him on TV for years and seen his vulnerability up close and personal were able to slow him down to theirs. Ebdon was one such being. He was so painstaking he made Thorburn look pacy.

The score stood at 12-12. There was one frame left to play. It was anyone's match. Or was it? As things worked out Jimmy didn't get a look-in, Ebdon closing him out with a 123 break that seemed to have been made by a man possessed. If you didn't know him better you'd have thought he was on drugs.

It ended with his trademark "Come on!", a phrase Ebdon used to gee himself up at key moments. Not that he needed to, what with those intense little eyes almost bulging out of their sockets, and the smile of a Roman emperor playing gently about his lips. (Ebdon's theatrical displays of emotion both before and after this event at moments of victory or near-victory have failed to endear him to the public, or indeed many of his colleagues.)

Jimmy, at least, had gone the distance instead of capitulating. Ebdon went on to beat Davis in the next round and then, agonisingly, Ronnie O'Sullivan, before falling to Hendry in the final, which was simply a bridge too far for him after all his exertions. It was Hendry's sixth world title, so he'd now equalled the modern day records set by both Reardon and Davis.

Jimmy's 1996/97 season wasn't much better. He lost in the first round of many tournaments: The Asian Classic (3-5 to Brian Morgan), the Grand Prix (1-5 to Tony Jones), the UK (7-9 to Tai Pichit) and the Welsh Open (3-5 to Dylan Leary). Mark Davis knocked him out at the qualifying stages of the German Open and John Higgins in Round Two of the European Open. He reached the quarter-final of the International, but again ran up against a brick wall in Hendry. Hendry also knocked him out of the Thailand Open in Round Two. John Higgins beat him 5-3 in the second round of the European Open and Dominic Dale won by the same score in the first round of the British Open. At Sheffield maybe he was still smarting from the close match with Ebdon the previous year as he didn't seem to be himself in the first round against Anthony Hamilton, losing 10-7 to the chagrin of the legion of fans who'd made the annual pilgrimage. Hamilton was a doughty break-builder and lethal among the balls. He never won a major title, but anyone in the game knew he was a handful and not to be taken for granted. Jimmy battled gamely, but didn't have enough in the tank. After the last ball was potted there were groans from the audience. Hamilton confessed, "I must be the most unpopular man in Sheffield." He wondered if anyone would put him up for the night.

That run of defeats meant Jimmy was now out of the top 16 for the first time in his professional career. His reaction to this turn of events? "I don't really care," he droned in a rare moment of public negativity. The pain of the past few years had finally risen to the surface.

I felt he was being beaten by people who weren't fit to lace his shoes – or even his whiskeys. He was the Big Gun, but he was being shot down too often to be funny. Stalked first and then executed. Summarily. The more he lost, the more losing became expected, became a habit. Like giving up cigarettes or drink, it was a hard one to kick.

It worked the other way too. Once somebody beat him, be it Mick Price or Nigel Bond or anyone else who seemed to have cracked some inner code of the White safe, they knew what beating him felt like. They knew how to handle it. It wasn't a big deal any more. The prospect of facing Jimmy White wasn't daunting the next time the referee flipped the coin. There was no need to be intimidated by Jimmy's achievements or reputation, still less his idolatry by the crowd. If anything that worked in his opponents' favour. They had less to prove. They could win ignominiously and still not be castigated because they were the self-appointed dullards, here to 'do a job' on Jimmy.

As time went on there was a horrifying inevitability to a White break ending prematurely. For no other reason than nerves, or history. You could almost script it in advance.

Not that Jimmy would admit it – to himself or publicly – but Snooker's Grim Reaper was sharpening his blade.

TOO MUCH LOVE

THE MOST EXCITING player to break onto the snooker scene in the 1990s was undoubtedly Ronnie O'Sullivan, the spiritual godson of Higgins and White. Hendry may have dominated the decade trophy-wise, but despite (or maybe because) of this, cult popularity eluded him.

Ronnie was impressed by Jimmy from their very first meeting at an Under-16s event in Birmingham in 1989 when Ronnie was 14. Jimmy was dressed in a pair of jeans and an old shirt and was also wearing an old pair of cowboy boots. Even then he had an entourage of five. Jimmy was friendly to Ronnie, which touched him as he was something of a legend then and Ronnie an unknown. According to Ronnie, "He was the first great player who came up and spoke to me like a human being."

Two years later, Ronnie came up against Jimmy in the European Open and beat him 5-1. Ronnie was on a roll at the time, having won most of the matches he played in trying to get on the pro circuit, and Jimmy a bit match-rusty. A few years later, in 1992, Ronnie was playing Cliff Wilson in the UK Championship and Jimmy put £4,000 on Ronnie to beat him. Wilson wasn't a positional player, but he was such a brilliant potter it hardly mattered. Jimmy once said, "He reminds me of Perrie Mans. The white ball flies around the table after almost every shot and nobody knows where it's going to end up, but somehow the break keeps going." Some people would say that sentiment applied to Jimmy too, at least in his very young days before he finessed his talent.

When the score went to 4-4 in the Wilson/O'Sullivan match, Jimmy came up to Ronnie and said, "Is there any fucking chance of you beating this fat, bald, half-blind geezer?" Ronnie was dumbstruck until he understood that Jimmy had put the bet on him. Knowing this disturbed his concentration and he lost the match 9-8. He was annoyed with Jimmy for letting him know that he'd bet on him. That put added pressure on his young shoulders.

The Rocket, as Ronnie became known, was to become the new generation's cult hero, with frailties to rival Jimmy's own, but when Ronnie self-destructed in matches it was for different reasons. He's as perfectionistic and bull-headed as Jimmy but he sets such high standards for himself that when the wheels come off, as they inevitably must at some time in every pursuit, he takes it out on himself.

If Jimmy goes into denial, Ronnie is guilty of excessive self-blame. They are like flipsides of the same coin. But if they could exorcise their demons maybe they'd also lose the motherlode from which they stripmine their inspirational tendencies. Of course Ronnie could get bored with snooker or frustrated with it, as he proved during a controversial walk-out during a match with Hendry when he was trailing 4-1

Ronnie firmly believes one of the reasons Jimmy never won the World title was because he placed too much emphasis on it to the detriment of other tournaments. He practised hard for Sheffield, but not hard enough for the rest of the snooker calendar. This meant that he was somewhat out of sorts coming to Sheffield and the 17-day ordeal eventually got to him in the six finals he lost. "It was as if no other tournament mattered," Ronnie said. "He wanted it so badly that in the end it did his brain in."

Ronnie echoed a familiar view when he said that Jimmy had "more ability than any other player I've ever seen," but technically speaking Jimmy was remiss by playing off that ability rather than any strategy he could have employed. Ronnie felt that if Jimmy had someone like Del Hill (Ronnie's former coach) in his camp it might have made all the difference. Ronnie's father once said of Hill, "If he told you to stick a cucumber up your arse and walk around the arena because it made you play well, you would."

Ronnie's overall view of Jimmy was that he lacked a proper endgame. "Look at Tiger Woods," he said. "When it comes down to the last nine holes in golf, they say that's where the tournament begins." Hendry used to say the same about Sheffield, or any other major, i.e. that the tournament only really started for him when he got the first round or two over. First round matches were often graveyards of favourites and Jimmy often fell off his horse in such rounds. In a best of nine, anybody could really beat anybody.

If the favourite went behind he was playing catch-up all the while, which affected his confidence, or willingness to take on dangerous pots. The result was that the underdog smelt fear and, having nothing to lose because he wasn't fancied, relaxed and went for everything. Often in such circumstances the balls started going in with alarming regularity. Or maybe Lady Luck smiled, as she usually tended to do, on the front-runner. Before you knew what was happening you were on the way home, suited and booted, having been dumped out of a prestigious tournament by a nobody.

The young Ronnie was beaten by Paul Hunter in Aberdeen once and tried to console himself by having a conversation with Jimmy, who'd also lost that night. "I just self-destructed," Ronnie said. "I'd really done myself up like a kipper." Jimmy knew how he felt. He told Ronnie he loved snooker when he was winning, but when he wasn't it was "a bastard of a game". He knew he had only six or seven years of playing left in him and wanted to make them count.

Shortly afterwards Jimmy told Jon Wilde of *Loaded* magazine, "Until I've got my hands on the world trophy, the rest of it counts for nothing. Every year that I miss out it gets harder and harder because talented new players are coming up all the time, but I can't accept that it will never be mine. It fucking tortures me. I've come so close so many times. If I get any closer, some bastard in the audience will probably pick up a gun and shoot me."

Wilde asked Jimmy how he felt about his image as a tearaway and Jimmy replied, "I'm more of a flier than a tearaway. I enjoy the good things in life and I can't see anything wrong with that. We all have our ways of letting off a bit of steam. Steve Davis gets a kick out of spending fortunes on records. Whenever I see him at airports he's always carrying these fucking huge boxes of records. That's what turns him on. As for myself, I like to wind down with a few drinks. That don't make me a tearaway, but I still get called a lovable rogue or whatever. I don't really mind. I'd rather people think I'm a lovable rogue than a total cunt."

Pressed about the comparison between himself and Higgins he said, "I don't really understand when I'm compared to him. He does like to grab himself a bit of attention, that boy, and that's not my style at all. If I ever pissed into a flower bowl at the Crucible I'd make sure no-one was watching. I'm not going to mug myself off. If I decide to take a piss in a public place I'm not going to ring for a video camera to record it for posterity." The main difference between himself and Higgins, he said, was that "he's out to fuck the system and I'm more interested in playing it. That doesn't mean I have to compromise myself. I won't take shit off anyone. I won't lick anyone's arse. But if you try to beat the system and you haven't got the right kind of back-up you'll end up completely fucked."

Shortly before this interview took place Jimmy had been arrested for the drink-drive offence I mentioned earlier (in his BMW he'd been found with four times the legal limit of alcohol in his system.) His solicitor argued that marital stress was the cause of his bingeing and the judge (a snooker fan?) thought it

Jimmy escaped a custodial sentence, instead receiving 120 hours of community service. The experience, he said, humbled him. "I was lucky I didn't go to jail," he admitted, "but more importantly I was lucky I didn't kill someone 'cos I was well over the top. I've spent 15 years working to get where I am. It would have been fucking stupid to have ruined it all in a moment of madness."

If losing was an Olympic sport, I thought, *Jimmy would have won gold*. He seemed to be able to contrive more ways of losing than the most ingenious player in the world could do of winning: leaving free balls when there was no need to, feathering the cue ball on a crucial break, even going in-off frame balls. His form improved somewhat in the 1997/98 season. He got to the semi-final of the Grand Prix, but was disappointingly beaten by Dominic Dale. He reached the third round of the UK, but Alan McManus was solid, thrashing him 9-3. Hendry didn't have much trouble beating him 5-2 in the first round of the German Open, and Rocket Ronnie O'Sullivan then beat him twice in succession, in the fourth round of the Scottish Open (5-3) and the third round of the Welsh (5-4). Hendry again proved too strong for him in the Thailand Open and disposed of him comfortably by a 5-2 margin.

Things got so bad Jimmy had to qualify for Sheffield, having fallen out of the top 16. He did so, but then, as qualifier, was unseeded and drew Stephen Hendry in the first round. Disaster.

I went into a bookie's office and asked for the odds on Hendry to win. I'd taken to betting against Jimmy to numb the pain of watching him lose. The Scot was 1/8. But Jimmy went 7-1 up on him. Hendry then reeled off three frames to go just 4-7 down. "It's not a crisis just yet," Clive Everton said from the commentary box as the nation tensed itself for yet another White capitulation, "but it's approaching one." I don't think there's any other player in the world who could be conceived of as being in a crisis while three frames in front except Jimmy. But then Clive Everton, like the rest of us, was all too aware of his inconsistencies. A few weeks before this match Jimmy had been beaten by an unknown called Mark Gray in Plymouth in the British Open. Gray was ranked 150th in the world.

At this point the BBC, in their wisdom, cut off transmission. "We stayed with it as long as we could," said David Vine as he bade farwell with pain in his eyes at letting down his viewers ... but they didn't. Not as far as I was concerned anyway. A boring programme followed and I started to panic.

I rented out a film to take my mind off the match. All radios were turned off for fear of a result coming on a news show as I hung in there for the highlights show that evening. I watched the film in a total daze. It was called *Smylla's Feeling For Snow*. That's about all I remember about it, except for the fact that Gabriel Byrne and Julia Ormond were in it. It could have been a masterpiece or it could have been a turkey; I wouldn't know. When it was over I looked at my watch: another half hour to go until the highlights programme. That half hour felt like five hours. Then Dickie Davis came on smiling and I felt this augured well. A few moments later he showed us the frame the BBC had cut off from earlier. So now I felt Jimmy had to have won. And indeed he had, by 10 frames to 4. Jimmy White had finally beaten Stephen Hendry.

I was over the moon. It was a measure of how many disappointments I'd suffered at Jimmy's hands that getting out of the first round at Sheffield, albeit against the multiple world champ, had such heady overtones.

In fact it was better than that, it was the greatest day of my sporting life.

So how did it happen? I don't really know, but the fact that Jimmy had been written off by all the journalists going into the match might have helped. He always likes to kick against the pricks. Being favourite unnerves him. He prefers to be the hunter rather than the hunted. Maybe Hendry was smug too. I didn't want to analyse it too much. I couldn't, I was too busy just savouring the moment.

The closest Jimmy had ever come to that kind of glory previously was when he demolished Davis in the World semi-final in 1990. There had been so many other occasions where I'd slouched to bed in deep depressions when he lost 5-4 after leading 4-0, or trailed 4-0 and then coming back to 4-4 before falling at the final hurdle. On such nights I have felt it necessary to tell people, "A national day of mourning will be declared tomorrow because Jimmy lost. All offices will remain closed to allow workers deal with their hangovers."

Jimmy put part of his victory down to a man called Mike Finnegan, who worked for a company specialising in positive thinking. He claims Finnegan helped him beat Hendry by teaching him how to visualise victory, or Hendry missing. It was like a self-prophetic fallacy. If you thought you'd win, you would. But how did that explain how many times Jimmy thought he'd win matches in the past and ended up on the wrong side of 5-4 scorelines ... or even 5-0 scorelines?

Maybe what Jimmy needed was somebody who specialised in negative thinking, not positive, to help him counteract his excessive abundance of confidence because to me his problem was that he failed to spot danger signals in matches. There was also the huge weight of expectation among the crowd, gathered to see him pull off yet more dazzling pots, and Jimmy heaped added pressure on himself by generally going for the tasty shot when a Davis-like safety would have been more savvy. Those people, myself among them, who roared out his name before or after (and sometimes even during) shots caused him eternal grief. Sometimes you can have too much love.

That victory over Hendry was so exciting that I bought a pair of surgical gloves to stop me biting my nails when Jimmy was playing in the next round. It became a ritual. People would come round to the house and say, "Aubrey's got his surgical gloves on. Jimmy must be playing". But after a while I ate into these too. I went through about a half dozen pairs before chucking them out.

Things even got to the stage where I started picking fights with people when he lost. I remember being in a pub one night where the barman turned off the programme and I went for him baldheaded. I wanted to haul him over the counter and beat him senseless. Fortunately (for both of us) I was so drunk I wasn't able to land a punch. I got off lightly by just being barred.

Ironically enough, Jimmy won that night.

It was just my luck not to see it. This made me think my attentions were giving him bad karma. Maybe if I forgot about him and went off to a desert island to meditate, he'd win all those World titles he once talked about, steamrollering his way past Hendry on his way to a hat-trick of trophies.

I knew I was in the minority with my obsession. I knew I was boring the pants off people talking about check side and drag and stun and *massé* shots when all they wanted to talk about was bridging loans, or how I was getting on teaching.

After the *Smylla's Feeling For Snow* experience, the next time the transmission cut off during a Jimmy match I started ringing up the sports departments of newspapers for results of matches. After a dozen or so calls like this people's patience tended to run thin. They might have been working on other articles and didn't like being interrupted. I got to know who was good-humoured and who not so in these vampire-like offices. Some people were surprised that I was always only interested in one man. Why did I want to know about White when a fellow countryman like Ken Doherty, who would one day win the world championship, was playing on another table?

I could pretend to be up for Doherty if he was playing Jimmy, and get the result that way. Or if Doherty and Jimmy were playing in two separate matches I'd ask for the Doherty result first to throw them off the scent and then casually interject, "Oh by the way, did White win?" (Usually he didn't.) I found it better in the long run to wait for the morning papers to get the result. Somehow you could cope with the depression better at dawn than dusk.

But I always felt Jimmy had a better chance of winning if I was watching. I could cheer him on even if I was watching a recording made while I was at work. It didn't make sense logically, but that was the way I felt. Equally if I was out and about I wouldn't hear any news of his progress to spoil my enjoyment of watching the match when I returned home. One day I was in a supermarket when a sports broadcast came on. I put my hands in my ears and started talking loud to myself to blot out the noise. The shopkeeper looked at me as if I was Jack Nicholson from *One Flew Over The Cuckoo's Nest*.

In 1996 Robert De Niro made a film called *The Fan*, which is a fascinating cautionary fable not only about how obsessive sport can become for people but also, even more importantly, how fans – let's not forget the term is shorthand for fanatics – can often be more affected by the fortunes of their idols than the idols themselves.

The stars, you see, are professionals, while the fans are amateurs. And often amateurs have more love for a game than those who earn their living from it. When you earn your living from something, by definition, it becomes a job: a career rather than a vocation. In an ideal world the two are combined, but this isn't an ideal world.

Robert De Niro plays Gil Renard, a knife salesman down on his luck, a kind of latterday version of Arthur Miller's Willy Loman from *Death of a Salesman*, frantically pedalling an outmoded sales pitch. When it stops working, he becomes like the Michael Douglas of *Falling Down*. His problems are compounded by his dysfunctional family set-up. The last straw is when his hero, Bobby Rayburn (Wesley Snipes), hits a poor patch on the baseball field. De Niro and Snipes, the film is at some pains to point out, are essentially very similar to one another, both in their perfectionistic temperaments and their seesaw circumstances.

Benicio Del Toro threatens Snipes's place on the team, but then he's murdered. Snipes's form now picks up. He hits a few home runs, much to the delight of De Niro. When the pair finally meet – courtesy of De Niro rescuing Snipes's son from drowning in one of the film's more unlikely developments – De Niro asks Snipes if his new-found form can be traced to Del Toro's demise. Snipes disagrees. All he will allow is that it had an indirect effect.

"I stopped caring after he died," he tells a bewildered De Niro. "I realised sport isn't that important, that it's not a cure for cancer."

He relaxed his arm, he says, and as a result his form came back and he started hitting.

This isn't what De Niro wants to hear. He wants Snipes to reassure him about the fact that the 11 strip reclaimed from Del Toro was what kickstarted his renaissance. Neither is De Niro impressed when Snipes tells him he doesn't care too much for his fans. "They love you when you're up," he says, "but when you're down they won't give you the time of day."

In the climactic sequence De Niro, outraged by Snipes's devil-may-care attitude to his art compared to his own deranged obsession, devises a plan to make his erstwhile idol have to play for his life: he kidnaps his son, demanding he hit a home run and dedicate it to him in order to set the beloved son free. Would I one day have to kidnap Jimmy's son Tommy to make Jimmy see sense?

Jimmy's second round opponent after beating Hendry was Darren Morgan. In my view anything from now on was a bonus. As it worked out Jimmy destroyed Morgan 13-3, still on a high from that first round victory. I knew it would have been asking too much for him to do a job on Ronnie O'Sullivan in the quarter-final so I didn't even let myself hope for that. Ronnie ran out a 13-7 victor. He was by now the real deal, the pretender who was about to take the throne. This was okay. A point had been proved. The people who wrote Jimmy off (myself among them) before the event had to eat their words.

O'Sullivan made the final, but lost to John Higgins. The Rocket would be back, though. His story was just beginning.

BEHIND THE WHITE BALL

JIMMY WROTE HIS autobiography in 1998. Or rather co-wrote it. His partner in this particular crime was one Rosemary Kingsland. On almost every page there were words like 'baroque', 'gravitate' and 'peccadilloes'. Clearly, this was Ms Kingsland attempting to usurp the natural charm of a lovable lad. Why had he let her do it? Maybe he hadn't even read the proofs. Jimmy himself tells us in the book that he can't read.

Did he do it (or have it done) for the money? It would be sad for someone like Jimmy to sell out for the 12 pieces of silver. Of course the timing was right. He'd been through so much since 1995 what with the deaths of his mother and brother, not to mention his own brush with the Big C. And of course his career was on the skids. But when he writes, as he does, that 'I want to tell it like it is, and like it really was,' I found myself unable to buy into this.

Where's the cocky cockney then? Where's the lovable rogue full of flash and zip, the wired kid who's so far off the edge he's almost back on again?

Ms Kingsland also has Jimmy 'instigating' mischief and indulging in something s/he calls 'the art of truanting'. The pity about the book is that even on the odd occasions that we're presented with the Jimmy we know and love, the language sanitises the events being catalogued out of all recognition. It's as if somebody put Little Lord Fauntleroy on Skid Row. Read this book and you start to wonder what you saw in the geezer in the first place. Because even though he goes on the razzle with Alex Higgins quite a bit in it, he sounds more like Steve Davis. And I don't mean Steve 'Interesting' Davis, I mean Steve 'Boring' Davis.

The book was called *Behind the White Ball*, a title that played with the American phrase 'Behind the eight ball', which is pool parlance for being in trouble. And yes, Jimmy is in trouble in the book a lot, as you would expect. But the main trouble is off the table. He doesn't really try to analyse why he lost six world titles except in semi-humorous vein when he writes about Mike Finnegan's analysis towards the end.

The book is best and truest to its subject in the passages dealing with Jimmy's marriage. These are the most entertaining – and revelatory – pages. Jimmy is glad Maureen doesn't play 'the little lady', but equally he has to face the music when she comes gunning for him. We're never in doubt about their relationship. The marriage is made in heaven, but then, as the man said, so is thunder and lightning. By the end of the book one feels Maureen is more likely to contemplate murdering Jimmy than divorcing him. As for him, she's like another one of his addictions.

My main problem with the book was with the language Jimmy uses. It's laughable to think of him using expressions like 'Lenny grinned conspiratorially' or 'He kept up an ecstatic mantra' as we get here. It just didn't ring true to the Jimmy I'd met (once in a blue moon!). Rhyming cockney slang was always more to this boy's liking than the King's English, but he put that on the back boiler here in a book that sucks the juice out of him even as it purports to capture him in freefall.

There was one thing that really intrigued me though. At one stage in the book Jimmy talks about a fan who did himself an injury while watching him play. I was wondering if that was a reference to myself.

Shortly after the book came out, Alex Higgins discovered he had contracted cancer of the palate. The year before he had been stabbed by a former girlfriend, Holly Haise, who he had also been violent with. The *Daily Express* rang Jimmy for Higgins's phone number and Jimmy took the opportunity to suggest they pay Alex £10,000 for an interview. The newspaper agreed to the fee, but Higgins still refused to talk to them.

Jimmy rang Higgins every other day to offer him support, telling him jokes to prop up his spirits and filling him in on the snooker gossip. Just this once the Whirlwind out-talked the Hurricane, whose cancer prevented him from speaking in anything beyond a whisper. "I used to be in stitches and pain at the same time," Higgins said afterwards about these calls. He appreciated Jimmy all the more because so many people in the game had turned their backs on him, largely due to his outrageous behaviour. But Jimmy would never forget the man who first inspired him and whose erratic temperament he also enjoyed, if not emulated.

Higgins subsequently started a legal action against the cigarette manufacturers who'd sponsored so many tournaments during his youth for glorifying smoking. This was hardly likely to succeed. It was a bit like Brendan Behan saying he was going to sue the Guinness brewery after contracting liver problems. Jimmy himself was glad that tobacco sponsorship of tournaments died out, and also that a smoking ban existed in public places. "It gives a better image of the game to the younger players," said the man who once smoked for England.

In November of that year Dawn Neesom interviewed Jimmy for the *Daily Star*. Her opening paragraph was ominous: 'Jimmy White is slumped in an armchair, a half-empty bottle in one hand, a dusting of dubious white powder on his waistcoat and a glazed look in his tired blue eyes.' In the next paragraph, however, she explained that the bottle contained milk, the white stuff was baby talc and the glazed look was the result of getting up in the middle of the night to feed his baby son Tommy Tiger.

Jimmy admitted he probably wasn't going to be quite the doting dad or baby bore yet, but considering he'd blown millions in his relatively short life he'd decided to slow down. "If you suggested to my Maureen that I'm a reformed character," he added with a grin, "she'd have hysterics." He said he already had Tommy Tiger booked into a posh school where he'd play golf instead of snooker. "You earn more money that way," Jimmy explained, "and if he takes after me, he'll need it!" Money was still a touchy subject, he admitted, but he'd mended his ways here too. "I allow myself a £5 accumulator bet on the football every Saturday and that's my lot."

His form had meant prize money from competitive snooker was drying up a bit, but he still had exhibitions and his book was bringing in a few nicker. He didn't drink much either, apart from a few glasses of bubbly the night Tommy was born. He was playing an exhibition match in Jersey when Maureen rang with the news. (Some things never change.)

Tommy, he revealed, had been conceived during a holiday in Bahrain where there was nothing else to do. He was a surprise to both of them, especially Jimmy after his testicular cancer. "Before the cancer, Maureen and I only had to look at each other and she'd fall pregnant," he joked. But all four previous children had been daughters. With Tommy, the White name would continue into the next generation.

Tommy Tiger wasn't named after golf sensation Tiger Woods, as many imagined. He got the name because he was born in the Chinese year of the Tiger, as indeed was Jimmy. The Tommy prefix was for Jimmy's dad.

Jimmy was also interviewed by Johnny Watterson in *The Times* that year, and the subject of his reformed character came up again. "I was a big drinker,"

Jimmy confessed. "I drank anything and everything. I get silly soppy drunk now, you know, ordinary drunk. Before, I'd be last to leave the bar and I'd have somewhere else to go. Bit of an animal, to be honest with you. I never needed a drink in the morning to function but I needed one to sleep. There was a time I wouldn't have been able to meet you until three in the afternoon, and only then with a pint of Guinness. Now I'm off on a Friday night practising. You wouldn't have caught me doing that a few years ago if I was paid."

Watterson asked him about his relationship with all the managers he'd had. "I've been ripped off by most of them," Jimmy said. "Most players get ripped off. It's because snooker players aren't the most intelligent people in the world. Even if they are, they don't have time. The game's too hard to concentrate on books and things."

Pressed about his own attitude to books, he admitted, "I had to teach myself to read because I was never at school. I can read a book, but if I don't get a word I get the whole thing wrong. If I was to write you a letter I'd make about fifty mistakes. But my calculations are good."

He continued to maintain, though, as was the case in most interviews he conducted around this time, and even the one with me from almost a decade before, that he was a reformed man: "I don't gamble. I can't do it no more. If I had £950 I used to borrow £50, so that I could have £1,000. I'm not proud of that. But I'm not bothered either. I'll get rich again and I'll win the World Championship."

Speaking more generally he said, "Snooker has improved 21 points since I was a teenager but I love the game. If they let me, I'll retire at 40 and play golf. I'm crap at it but I love that too."

Well, Jimmy didn't retire at 40 and he didn't win the World Championship, but one had to commend his fighting spirit and belief.

Jimmy's 98/99 season was up and down. Shokat Ali beat him in a close match in Round One of the Grand Prix. He reached the third round of the UK, but was soundly thrashed 9-2 by the emerging Paul Hunter. Ebdon beat him in both the Scottish and Irish Masters, and Ronnie O'Sullivan in the second round of the Welsh Open. In the qualifying round of the Thailand Open he went down to a total unknown in Hugh Abernathy. He also went out in the qualifying round of the China Open, to Jonathan Birch and John Parrott beat him 5-4 in the second round of the British Open. That just left Sheffield, but he went out in the first round to Alan McManus. McManus is a good player, but he shouldn't be putting Jimmy White out of World Championships. Not at this early stage anyway. It was as if the Scot smelt blood from the off. Every ball he potted was like another nail in the coffin of Jimmy's career. The crowd droned and moaned. McManus had become Public Enemy Number 1, like so many of Jimmy's previous conquerors. The shame was this was now an annual event, or so it seemed.

Jimmy played for England in the Nations Cup in 1999. He didn't perform well personally, but the team still won due to sterling efforts from the likes of Ronnie O'Sullivan, Stephen Lee and John Parrott. Jimmy didn't attend the celebration party, feeling he'd let the side down. Ronnie felt for him. "It was a team effort," he said to console him, "and you were the fucking bollocks." Ronnie's belief was that Jimmy's presence lifted the morale even if he wasn't the player he had once been.

But, no matter how many claims he made about turning over a new leaf wherever Jimmy went, trouble was soon to follow. He was simply too big a name, with too long a history, for journalists to miss out on. Ronnie and Jimmy were together in Thailand that year when the *News of the World* sent out two journalists to try and find some juicy gossip on them cavorting with the local talent there. Ronnie was spotted with a woman in his room, though he insists she wasn't a prostitute. He pleaded with the journalists not to stitch him up because he was engaged to be married at the time, but they didn't listen. Jimmy was also namechecked in the article and Ronnie was enraged. The next time he spotted the journalist he threw a bucket of ice-cold water over him.

Conversely, Jimmy's achievements in the game of snooker were recognised by another, more reputable part of the British establishment. He was awarded an MBE and was chuffed to pieces to receive it. Ironically, the other players who have MBEs are those who've beaten him in finals at Sheffield: Hendry, Davis and Parrott.

The award perked up his game, if only for a while. In May 1999 he won through to the final of the Riley Premier League after a surprise 6-1 throttling of Ronnie O'Sullivan in the semis. (It had been only the sixth time he got the upper hand on the Rocket in 17 meetings up to this point.) He was up against John Higgins in the final, but not feeling too good about it as Higgins had won their last seven encounters. The wily Scot won this one as well, with a comprehensive 9-4 scoreline. Higgins had something to prove as he'd just lost the World semi-final to Mark Williams. The match stood poised at 4-4 and Jimmy should have gone 5-4 up, but missed a brown with the rest in the ninth frame because he was over-stretching. After Higgins took that frame he coasted ahead, going through Jimmy for a shortcut.

As a consolation, Jimmy ended the 98/99 season by winning the Pontins Professional title. It wasn't a major, but it was the first time he'd held anything significant aloft since winning the Matchroom League in 1993 and it felt good. The conditions weren't ideal or there were doors slamming in the background as well as children screaming and the droning of a racing game in the arcade as he played. The Blue Coats eventually restored calm and Jimmy won a nip and tuck final against Matthew Stevens, the highlight being his 134 in frame 8 to forge 5-3 ahead. He ran out a 9-5 winner with some solid breakbuilding. Perhaps there was life in the old dog yet.

INSIDE THE MIND OF A

CHAMPION

SNOOKER ISN'T LIKE other games in the sense of peak physical fitness being required, or certain psycho-motor skills. A lot of it is intuition, the way you feel about yourself. The times when things aren't equal is when pressure causes your radar to go on the blink. Matches have been turned round on these crucial moments, which is why snooker makes better soap opera than, say, soccer or golf. There are heroes and villains, nemeses and hamartias, catastrophic blunders and chickens coming home to roost. I saw Jimmy as one of the classic blunderers, but still I couldn't stop watching him.

Meanwhile I continued to play snooker myself in the league. I was actually the captain of the team now. The joke was that they offered me the captaincy because I was the only one with a car. Without me they couldn't get to the matches. A lot of the nights we played in some real dead-end dives. I usually needed a drink to warm up, maybe two. You met some hard nuts at these bar counters. Also some rough women. We would trade insults, sometimes about my snooker prowess, or lack of it.

"You want to get yourself another hobby, boy," a guy said to me in a pub one night. It was just after I'd lost a match and I threw a punch at him. The bartender intervened and said I was barred. "He started it," I said. But I couldn't expect to be treated lightly in this man's local. Years before I had been barred from another pub in similar circumstances. Another night I lost my licence from driving under the influence and crashing into another vehicle. One of my first thoughts when I sobered up the next morning was that I would now have no way to get to Goffs for the Irish Masters. I had strange priorities in those mad years.

Drink was both disease and cure as far as I was concerned, disease because it made me not care enough on the shot, cure because when the game was over you had a balm to put over the wound. And maybe someone to drown your sorrows with. The bottle never argued, never told you that you should have put more side on the white, or trickled up behind the yellow in that tense last frame. The bottle was your friend. At least until the next morning when another kind of duty beckoned – like a job.

I knew my career as an amateur player was going down the toilet. Maybe my life was going down the toilet, period. Who cared? Not me. When you had enough in the tank it didn't matter (I mean booze, not petrol.) But driving was a worry too. Was I over the limit? Would I be caught again? What was I doing to my insides?

There's a saying that goes: when you lie down with the dogs you get up with the fleas. I made some bad friendships in these years, years I'd like to buy back now, years that robbed my health and whatever minute talent I tried to finetune against the odds in grotty venues where the odds were usually stacked against me anyway by 'friends' of my opponents. If they weren't cooking the scoreboard they were trying to cook me. After a while I stopped caring. If it meant that much to them let them have it. It didn't to me. And maybe that was the problem. To succeed in anything you needed to be obsessed by it. Like Jimmy. But he had a block too, and he liked his drink. Were the two things connected with both of us? I had a cheek thinking about myself in the same breath as him, but that was the way my mind worked at that time.

With a few pints of Smithwicks inside me I was a World finalist in my mind. I'd always been a dreamer and drink intensified that quality. It made my most intangible dreams realisable, just a whisper away. The worse I played the better I felt I could play. It was crazy, meaningless.

Mary railed at me for over-imbibing, and for acting like this insanity all mattered. She was practical. She knew what things were important: the job, my peace of mind, sanity. I saw these as tradeable commodities when I was under the influence. And sometimes even when I wasn't.

"Do I not matter?" she'd plead. For me it was a non-question. It wasn't that she didn't matter, but I could only focus on one thing at a time. A part of me wanted to be nuts, to be in love with the impossible dream, like Jimmy. To rejoin the real world meant making too many compromises. Life was easier with the bums and the losers. They didn't nag you into submission like the people who loved you. In that they were like the bottle.

Other nights it wasn't so bad. I didn't miss shots the World number 97 would have got with his eyes closed. I didn't insult my mates on the way home. I didn't drink one over the eight and risk losing my licence … again.

But something wasn't right. With my game or my life. Or both. Okay, I couldn't be Jimmy White. Who could? Maybe even Jimmy White couldn't be Jimmy White. That wasn't what it was about.

I had a job. Sometimes. I could string a few words together. Everyone was put on the planet for a different reason. I shouldn't have to feel I had to bend it like Beckham. Or Jimmy. Or anyone else for that matter. I was me, just as you are you. But I couldn't let my obsession lie.

Having heroes was what complicated the issue. It meant there was a lack of fulfilment at my core. My obsession with Jimmy meant I wasn't happy with who I was. But I kept on keeping on. Filling in the dots at work and in the evenings sucking on a beer and trying to attain dime-store grandeur by potting five balls in a row in Dublin in a building that could have been mistaken for somewhere the Sopranos might have hung out on an off-day. It was my lot to be a 2nd XI sort of guy. I had no right to expect more. To him to whom much was given much would be expected. But I had been born without a discernible talent. Maybe my talent was the ability to spot it in others, like Jimmy. Or to stop them doing their thing. That was it – I was a killjoy. All journalists were. They specialised in doing people down, finding their Achilles heel.

Most people would have killed to have a quarter of Jimmy's talent. Did it matter that he pissed most of it away? I'd often said to non-believers that the part of him that pissed it away was the same part of him that had it to piss in the first place. That was the conundrum. It was why people like Marilyn Monroe and James Dean also self-destructed. And any doomed rock-God you cared to mention, like Jimi Hendrix or Jim Morrison.

Was Jimmy in that league? Maybe Ronnie Wood would think so. Jimmy liked to be at the edge of that kind of dissolution, and some of it bled into his game. But I wasn't so I had no right to think I was entitled to such excesses.

I had once made a joke to somebody during a tennis match that I had similarities to John McEnroe. "I share his temper tantrums," I said, "but I can't play tennis." Equally I had Jimmy's brittleness, but not his genius. So what. Every Johnson needed a Boswell. I could be that at least. If he'd let me. But so far he was keeping me at arm's length, probably because he didn't think I had street cred. I was just this demented Paddy who made a habit of pestering him for interviews that never happened.

The world was my oyster, but an oyster was my world. Still, I had to grab at it because it was all I had. And in the meantime I had to try and prop up a dead-end team going fast nowhere under my ridiculous captaincy.

I didn't believe in my team. I didn't believe in me. Even if we topped the league, who cared? It was mickey mouse, chickenfeed. We were the minions of snooker, the unheralded foot-soldiers. We were in the gutter, and not even looking at the stars. But when that was all I had I made myself put up with it. And sometimes, just sometimes, it was enough.

There was a song Mary sang called 'To Win Just Once'. It was written by the Saw Doctors, a Galway group, about football. Galway had won the All-Ireland Football Championship a number of times, both in hurling and Gaelic. That made Mary feel good because it was her home county. My own county, Mayo, hadn't won the All-Ireland since 1951, two years before I was born. We had come close a few times in the mid to late 1990s, but, like Jimmy White, we snatched defeat out of the jaws of victory. Was this to be my destiny, to be forever associated with losers?

I listened to the Saw Doctors singing 'To Win Just Once' and felt carried away with the great emotion of the song. It came from a profound part of them and it carried a profound message. Some counties of Ireland, like Kerry for instance, had won the championship so often they almost felt like it was a God-given right to be presented with the trophy (a bit like Davis in snooker). But when you were Mayo, or Jimmy, to win just once would have been enough. It would have been something to tell the grandchildren, something to affirm your existence.

Sometimes, though, in life things didn't work out like that. Shit happened. Sometimes you were the pigeon and sometimes the statue. Was it Lady Luck? The golfer Gary Player used to say, "The more I practise, the luckier I get." I wasn't good at practising. Neither was Jimmy. (Were Mayo?) Maybe we all liked the stage, but the stage let us down – because we let it down. In years to come I would meet another snooker player, Ronnie O'Sullivan, who would win three world titles. Like Jimmy he was an attacking player and an unpredictable one. Unlike Jimmy he had a temper and would sometimes give up on matches that weren't going his way. Like Jimmy he was a perfectionist.

But the world wasn't perfect. Which meant that players like Ronnie and Jimmy were destined to suffer when the tricks of fate conspired to make jigsaws that missed seminal pieces, or re-jigged the gameplan to fuck them up. It was in the nature of things. It was Murphy's (White's?) Law. And some were better at dealing with it than others.

As they played, so also did they live. Wild on the table and wild off it. Two rock stars in the wrong professions. Jimmy should have been in the Rolling Stones and Ronnie should have been playing soccer for Arsenal, or golf with his hero Tiger Woods, or even tennis with another hero, Roger Federer. What went wrong? Why did they settle for the claustrophobic ambience of snooker? Was it all due to a childhood hobby gone west? Could the same be said for me? Maybe it was all about introversion. Most snooker players were introverts. It wasn't a team sport. It might even have been designed for depressives. Ask Alex Higgins. But when you were in the heat of battle you felt anything but an introvert. You felt like a Viking warrior sweating blood for your inch of turf.

* * *

Jimmy got back into the top 16 in the 2000/01 season thanks mainly to an appearance in the British Open final. He lost to Peter Ebdon, but being at the business end of a tournament again after such a long drought was a massive fillip. There were other reassuring signs. He reached the semis of the Grand Prix, where he was beaten 6-2 by Mark Williams. Nick Dyson beat him in the fifth qualifying round of the UK. Thereafter his form began to dip. Stephen Lee beat him 5-1 in round two of the China Open, but then Jimmy wasn't renowned for his form on foreign soil. He lost 5-1 to Ken Doherty in the first round of the Thailand Masters, 6-4 to Alan McManus in the first round of the Irish Masters and 5-3 to Stephen Maguire in the fifth qualifying round of the Scottish Open.

Something else was to hit him harder, though, than any of those disappointments, for the season ended with him not appearing at Sheffield. Jimmy's earlier bad form had meant he was forced to qualify for the 2001 event, but he and was knocked out by the promising Dubliner Michael Judge in the pre-televised stages.

No Whirlwind at the Crucible. Should I open a vein?

Ronnie O'Sullivan won his first World title that year. "It was a monkey off my back," the Rocket admitted. He'd been blitzing the opposition in every tournament you cared to mention since the early-80s and some people in the game had dubbed him 'the new Jimmy White' in the sense of being a Sheffield Nearly Man. But now that tag was a thing of the past. Jimmy was glad for him, but the victory had to make him feel his own lack of fruition all the more.

Ronnie said after his victory, "When I saw Jimmy being introduced to the crowd beforehand I just told myself not to end up like him by not winning this one." It sounded like a dispassionate brushing aside of his sometime idol, but in a way what he had done was win it for Jimmy.

When Ronnie had reached the semi-final of the World Championships in 1996 Jimmy rang him in his hotel room and told him he was playing fantastic stuff and if he got to the final Jimmy would be down to see him play. As it happened he lost, but Ronnie was still touched by the gesture. After Jimmy lost to the aforementioned Michael Judge five years later his first reaction was to think of his protégé. "All I want now is for Ronnie to go ahead and win it," he said. Jimmy was on holiday during the championships, but vowed to cut the holiday short if Ronnie got to the final. When he did, and was sitting in his dressing room waiting for the evening session on the first day to start, Jimmy arrived with Ronnie Wood and wished him the best of luck. Again Ronnie was touched.

The following day O'Sullivan became world champion, which rubbed things in for Jimmy. But according to Ronnie he didn't show his disappointment. That's why so many players feel for him, and why they often say – even to camera – that if they don't win the title, the person they want to see winning it most is Jimmy.

A few years ago, tired of being ignored by Jimmy, and hearing that Ronnie was coming to Dublin to play in an exhibition match, I rang the hotel he was staying in and got on to his manager. He agreed that I could speak to Ronnie no problem. I think I felt that if I got to know Ronnie a bit better I could work Jimmy out of my system.

After all the capering around after interviews with Jimmy, this seemed a bit too easy, so I half expected a no-show. However, when I turned up at Bewley's Hotel Ronnie was waiting for me. He spoke to me as if I'd known him all his life. Here was the world champion, the hottest property in the game and he was this accessible. I had to pinch myself. I sat down beside him and we chatted like two old friends. I vowed to myself that I would get to the bottom of why Ronnie had become world champion, while Jimmy had shot himself in the foot so often.

"All I wanted to do as a child was play the game," Ronnie told me. "I made a century at ten. Nobody had done that before at that age. It was a buzz. It gave me the passion. They told me I was a natural. Good hand-eye coordination. Five years later my dad built me my own table at the bottom of our garden. I played Eugene Hughes there. He was the first top pro I practised with. Then came Ken [Doherty]. I was playing on my instinct really. I didn't have any technique then, but I didn't seem to need one. It was only a few years later, when things started to go wrong, that I realised I needed something to fall back on. I needed a B game, something to win on even when I wasn't playing to my best. I think I'm getting that now. I used to drop my shoulders and tell myself it wasn't my day. That's gone now. I'm hungrier. I'll battle."

Ronnie is his own fiercest critic, setting sometimes unreachable goals to attain, often accusing himself of shoddy performances even when he wins tournaments. He's threatened to retire more times than Frank Sinatra. This is due to his perfectionism. "Even when I make lasagne," he said, "it has to be the best lasagne." He knows there's really only one player in the world who can beat him: himself. When that happens, he gets depressed.

I asked Ronnie how he felt about Jimmy. "Jimmy's a good lad," he said. "We've had some fun together over the years. We both play the same kind of game. He was thrilled when I won the World Championship."

Was he Ronnie's hero growing up? "Of course, but he didn't win enough. That was the problem. Davis did, so I started to follow him. I wanted to play like Jimmy and win like Davis. That's always been my ambition. And still is."

Ronnie revealed to me that he felt bad for Jimmy when he visited him in his dressing room following the Rocket's world title triumph in 2001. "I felt like giving him the trophy," he said. "I wanted to hand it to him and tell him to have it for a year just to see what it felt like. If I'd finished my career and never won it there would always have been a cloud over me. I'd never know if I was good enough."

We ran out of time then, but I offered to take Ronnie to the airport to catch a plane and he accepted. I was honoured that he would entrust this mission to me. I've never had a world champion in my car and I doubt I ever will again. Mary, who's no snooker buff, also felt honoured to carry his cue to the car. On the way to the airport, Ronnie took two calls on his mobile, both from his father, convicted of the murder on the Isle of Sheppey of the bodyguard of Charlie Kray, brother of the Kray twins, in 1992, who was phoning from his cell. Listening to a World snooker champion speaking to his East End dad in a prison cell from the back seat of a Fiat Uno is quite a surreal experience. I felt I was in the middle of a B-movie.

"He's the reason behind my success," Ronnie said after he put the phone down. "If it wasn't for him I wouldn't be sat here today. He was a tough taskmaster, never accepting second best. Whenever I won a tournament he never let me sit back on my success. He was always pushing me harder – so much so that eventually I couldn't have him at tournaments with me. It hurt me too much to miss, or lose. I was too self-conscious knowing he was watching my every move."

It struck me that no such figure had existed in Jimmy's life. Was that the difference between Ronnie and Jimmy? Was that the reason why O'Sullivan had won the World title, while Jimmy had come up short so many times?

It was clear to me the pair were mirror images of one another. Not least in their personable nature and attitude. Ronnie wrote his autobiography in 2003. I asked the publishers for a review copy and when it arrived I saw he'd written a little message on the inside cover: 'To Aubrey and Mary. Nice meeting you both. Lots of love, Ronnie xxx.'

A sweet gesture from a sweet guy.

Jimmy never emulated Ronnie's glory at Sheffield despite all the promises that he would, but in 2003 Jimmy won the Ladbrokes Poker Million, Britain's most prestigious poker tournament. He scooped a cool £80,000 for his labours, thereby showing the world that all those hours in hotel rooms between matches weren't totally wasted. He was up against the Hendon Mob, a group of seasoned players, comprising Joe 'The Elegance' Beavers, Tony 'The Lizard' Bloom, Bruce 'Elvis' Atkinson and Barney 'Barmy' Boatman. He was a 100-1 outsider when the competition began and 8/1 when it got down to the last six. Jimmy had two crucial wins on last card turns to scoop the $150,000 prize on 15 March before a huge Sky Sports television audience.

Perhaps the win was fitting for the harum-scarum card sharp. He'd always had a poker face at the snooker table. Wasn't it Willie Thorne who'd said, "You never know after a Jimmy match if he's won or lost if you visit him in the dressing room."? That's what people loved most about him: the grace with which he took defeat. There were never excuses, never Higgins-like scapegoating of referees, bad kicks or rubs of the green. It was always just, "I didn't produce." But now he had. It didn't take dexterity of the hand to be served a good one, but he'd played them mighty well and landed the bounty. Who was it that said we only succeed at what we do second best in life? Yes, this was poor consolation for Sheffield but it was still half a loaf. At least he was champion at something.

Viewers were given the chance to see all the players' strategies during the tournament as all cards were visible as a result of cameras placed under glass panels on the tables. Each player was also wired up to a heart monitor so viewers could also see how nervous they were. Jimmy attributed his success to all the hours he spent practising at Ladbrokespoker.com. He said he was going to celebrate his win by (you've guessed it) "having a game of poker tomorrow".

He seemed nerveless at poker. In fact the game even steadied him, helped him wind down. In snooker if your hand shook through nerves it wrecked the shot. Here it might have the opposite effect by throwing the other players off. Not that Jimmy's would have shaken. Neither could his courage at the poker table be punished by a Davis or a Hendry. Here gambling was rewarded – within reason. He found a new identity for himself at this table, calling things as he saw them, reaping the rewards of his decisions almost without moving. Suddenly, the struggling card player from *The Cincinnati Kid* had become The Man.

WHITE RIOT

THE 1999/2000 SEASON started brightly for Jimmy. He reached the third round of the British Open, but here he was amazingly whitewashed by Nick Walker (who he?). James Wattana beat him by the odd frame in the fourth round of the Grand Prix, as did Mark Williams in the fifth round of the UK. But at least he was at the business end of tournaments again. In the qualifying round for the China Open – one of his bogey tournaments – he was knocked out 5-3 by Wayne Brown. He got to the semi-final of the Welsh only to have his spirit quashed by Stephen Lee in a hard-fought match that Lee took 6-5. Ronnie O'Sullivan was more conclusive in beating him 5-1 in the second round of the Malta Grand Prix, as was Billy Snaddon in knocking him out of another bogey tournament for him, the Thailand Masters. Marcus Campbell beat him 5-4 in the third round of the Scottish Open as well.

Then came the 2000 World Championships. While Hendry was being knocked out by an unfancied Stuart Bingham in the first round, Jimmy beat the Scot Billy Snaddon, but a huge storm kicked off after Snaddon complained that Jimmy's supporters were over-vociferous during the match, which interfered with his concentration. The White fans cheered when Snaddon missed a pot or went in-off and cheered even more wildly when Jimmy scored, even when it wasn't a particularly brilliant shot. "It has nothing to do with Jimmy," Snaddon was careful to add, "He's one of the nicest guys on the circuit, but some of those people wanted throwing out. I don't think anybody out there wanted me to win."

Jimmy, protective of his doting fans, wasn't impressed by Snaddon's comments. "If some of these players went for a few balls instead of playing safe, then they'd get a few fans too," he accused. "I take chances and the punters like it. It's been my style from the first day I played the game and it's the way the people want it. I won't stop." He beat Bingham 13-9 in the second round, but this match was also characterised by the tribal loyalties of the fans to Jimmy. They were, admittedly, at their most extreme at this time.

In the opening frame, after Bingham had missed a brown, a spectator threw a piece of chewing gum wrapped in tinfoil in Bingham's direction. "It didn't hit me," Bingham said, "but you've got to think some of the crowd are out of order. You're not just playing Jimmy, you're playing them as well."

Could Jimmy be blamed for his followers? Hardly. Surely this was a matter for referees to deal with. Some players thrived on playing Jimmy even (especially?) when the crowd was partisan. Davis said it made him try harder. Hendry loved silencing them with brilliant play. Doherty said he relished playing Jimmy "in his own backyard", whether that meant London or the Crucible, which became a kind of home from home for him each April as legions of fans flocked to Sheffield to roar on their hero. It all probably hinged on the experience of his opponent. Often, Jimmy said, the people who cheered excessively for him disturbed his own concentration.

After winning these two matches Jimmy's odds to win the World title plummeted from a pre-tournament 40-1 to 12-1. Guy Hodgson commented in the *Independent*: 'Jimmy White at 12-1? This is a man who last won a ranking tournament eight years ago, who last prevailed at any event in June 1993 and who has made it to the final at the Crucible six times and not won. He can't win here.'

Hodgson's words proved prophetic as Jimmy was dumped out in the quarter-final by Matthew Stevens. Jimmy told the press, "I missed a very simple black in the seventh and I never really got into it from then on." Asked if he now contemplated retiring he was quick to quash that thought: "There's no way I'll quit. I still love competing. On top form I can win competitions." He still had the old bravado, but the bottom line was that he was again out of the '16' and from now on would have to pre-qualify for tournaments. Was it the beginning of the end for the mercurial genius?

Jimmy's form continued to be erratic as the new millennium gathered pace. Having fewer matches to play meant he wasn't getting much table time. He was never renowned for his love of practising but exhibition matches (for which he was perenially in demand) helped him keep his hand in. These generally garnered huge numbers of White devotees. Devotion, however, isn't worth much when you've just been booted up the backside by a mediocrity after unpacking your bags in some provincial hotel. The word was out on Jimmy for many years that you could beat him by unnerving him, which meant that he went into most tournaments with that Indian sign over him.

After a patchy 2001/02 season Jimmy returned to Sheffield in April 2002 and hammered Dominic Dale 10-2 in the first round. But Matthew Stevens then trounced him 13-3 in the second. Jimmy was dejected at how poorly he'd played, particularly since he'd had a good season (he was up to tenth in the provisional rankings.) "I lost the plot," he said mournfully afterwards. "When I got in the balls I seemed to get kicks and bad kisses and it all went west. I don't know what went wrong. I had chances, but if you don't take them with these young guns you're going to get murdered."

There was one incident in the match which shocked me even more than the heavy defeat. Jimmy was just six points behind and on a break. There were three reds left and he was playing a black off its spot, a bit like the one he missed against Hendry in 1994. He missed it and as it rebounded off the cushion he re-hit the white (which he'd screwed back towards his cue arm) back into it, causing both balls to jump off the table. It was a show of temper one might have associated with Higgins on a bad day, or somebody like Stephen Maguire in the modern game. But Jimmy White?

Viewers were astounded. Maybe 20 years of frustration went into that one gesture. He was finally ridding himself of the poker face and admitting how much he cared. In a way I felt good. I didn't think a man who lost six World finals should implode as much as he did. It couldn't have been good for his mental health.

Jimmy issued a statement of apology afterwards to both viewers and fans. "It was completely out of character," he said. "I can't believe what I did. I don't even do that in practice."

After a much-needed break, the 2002/03 season boded better. Jimmy reached the semi-finals of both the UK Championship and the Masters at Wembley so he wasn't going to hang up his cue just yet, contrary to what the sports 'experts' predicted in the newspapers. At the end of the season the British government's anti-tobacco legislation was enforced, which spelt the end of Regal sponsoring either the Welsh or Scottish Open, and also Benson & Hedges funding the Masters. This fact, coupled with falling viewer figures and the dearth of 'characters' in the game – many of the up-and-coming pros looked like tailor's dummies and spoke about as much – threatened the future of the game. The WPBSA fell under much criticism from people like Clive Everton, the BBC commentator and editor of *Snooker Scene* magazine.

The game was also tainted by the whiff of cordite surrounding Jeffrey Archer, whose tenure as president of the WPBSA ended with his conviction for perjury by a London court, as did his mayoral ambitions for that city. In the absence of tobacco manufacturers other sponsors for events were desperately sought, but the number of tournaments on the circuit were shortened and fears were expressed by all and sundry that the game was dying on the vine.

"We need a Simon Cowell to re-energise it," Ronnie O'Sullivan opined as he made off to foreign shores to play pool. Steve Davis felt the future lay in places like China. Ding Jun Hui failed to capitalise on his early promise as a *wunderkind* and possible teenage world champion, but other players like Liang Wenbo, who caused something of a stir at the 2008 World Championships, were coming through. Sir Rodney Walker, who took over from Archer at the helm of the WPBSA, promised to do everything he could to renew the high media profile the game had had during the heady days of the 1980s.

But then came an announcement no-one had seen coming. In 2003, Maureen announced that she was finally divorcing Jimmy. True, what surprised most people was that they'd lasted so long together. The marriages of people like Davis, Hendry and Doherty were solid, like their game, but Jimmy had always seemed like a marital accident waiting to happen. In this, as in most other things, he was like Higgins – Alex, that is, not John. The latter man has stability both in his game and home. Undoubtedly one bleeds into the other. On the other hand, relatively quiet men like John Virgo, Willie Thorne, Neal Foulds, Dennis Taylor and Ray Reardon were also divorced. Foulds's wife controversially deserted him for a bingo caller. Thorne lost his wife as a result of a gambling addiction and subsequent bankruptcy. Reardon left his wife after 26 years. Virgo split in 1991. Taylor dumped his wife for a woman 16 years younger than him.

Said Clive Everton, "Snooker marriages certainly seem to be more accident-prone than those in other sports. The lifestyle isn't conducive to homespun harmony. For a start, top players can be away for up to 200 days a year. And every match demands long periods of high concentration which leads to stress. Golfers have that too, and so do tennis players. The difference with snooker players is that they're often playing late into the night. There's no space at the end of the day to relax."

In other sports the players wives – they would come to be known as WAGS in the noughties – accompanied their husbands to tournaments. Snooker wasn't like that. "Jimmy's always said that playing snooker makes him feel alive," Everton continued. "Without that adrenalin flow, when he's sitting around doing nothing, he feels half dead. He's one of the lucky few who's got to the top on natural talent, but he can't burn the candle at both ends forever."

For all that, over the previous five or six years the White's marriage had seemed as stable as at any time in their relationship. Perhaps they simply realised there was nowhere else left to go.

Matthew Norman gave a fitting endnote to Jimmy when he wrote in the *Guardian*: 'His marriage has suffered grievously from his habit of nipping out for a pack of fags and returning a week later with no memory of anything beyond the first 27 pints.'

Did the divorce change Jimmy? The early evidence was that, unlike the bereavements which had visited him in the mid-90s, this knockback gave him more focus on his game. Following his poker victory in 2003, Jimmy made history of a different sort in the Players Championship that year where he played his snooker with more determination than he'd done for years. It had already been a good season for him coming up to this event as he'd reached the final of the European Open and the semi-finals of both the UK Championship and the Masters. In fact Jimmy earned more ranking points in the 2003/04 season than anyone else bar Ronnie O'Sullivan. This was in stark contrast to 2002/03 in which he failed to win even a single ranking point.

Looking at him you felt as if the fire was back in his belly. He beat Ian McCulloch 5-3 in the quarter-finals. This was a tight match which looked like going to a decider as McCulloch, trailing 3-4, but on a break of 49 in the 8th frame, seemed set to square the match. But when a black jangled in the jaws of the pocket, Jimmy made a brilliant 57 to reach the semis. There he met Peter Ebdon. As one might have expected, this was also a gruelling encounter. At 5-4 up, Ebdon looked a dead cert to beat Jimmy in their best-of-11, but in the 10th frame he potted a blue and red simultaneously to let Jimmy in. Jimmy levelled, and eventually won the match in an agonisingly slow decider that went all the way to the pink. The match lasted nearly four hours and Jimmy got a standing ovation when the last ball went in. His fans were beginning to truly believe once again.

The final of the Players Championship, against Paul Hunter, was a comedy (or tragedy) of errors. Hunter led only once in the match, at 5-4. At this point Jimmy raced ahead, winning the next four frames in less than an hour. Hunter made a 67 in the next and took the 15th on the black to set the alarm bells ringing in Jimmy's head. But he held his nerve to close things out with a 49 break in the last frame.

As the last ball went down, Jimmy was hugged both by Hunter and his 84-year-old dad before entering the winner's enclosure, a relieved grin etched on his features. At 42, he had become the oldest man since Doug Mountjoy won the Mercantile Credit Classic in 1989 to win a ranking tournament. It was also his first major tournament victory in 12 years. No other player had ever achieved that feat of such a long gap between ranking victories. He had now won ranking events in three separate decades and had also accumulated 450 ranking points in the season, pushing him up to 10th in the world.

Asked about the overall standard of the error-strewn match, Jimmy concluded, "We played like a couple of amateurs. I can't believe how many balls we missed." He admitted that the continual need to focus on ranking points had eaten into his concentration. Now he could chill out, relax and go to the Crucible with one less thing on my mind. "That's just magic because I haven't been able to do it in years," he said. Was Jimmy back in the big time? Could I pin my hopes on him again?

"I just keep on punching," he said afterwards, echoing the words of the boxer Roberto Duran, who had that as his motto. It was almost like a mantra for Jimmy, and a frequent comment in interviews he conducted over the years both in victory and defeat. Jimmy had learned to treat those two 'imposters' just the same, as Rudyard Kipling advised in his poem *If*.

"I'm just delighted to get this out of my system," beamed a jubilant Jimmy. "I'm absolutely knackered, totally wiped out. It hasn't sunk in yet. I'm so used to losing I can't get my head around the fact that I've got the trophy. It's a phenomenal feeling." With ten ranking tournament titles under his belt it brought him to joint sixth with John Parrott on the all-time ranking list behind Hendry, Davis, Williams, John Higgins and Ronnie O'Sullivan.

His defeated final opponent, Paul Hunter, was one of life's true gentlemen, a lad who loved going off the rails with pranks between tournaments. He was also a doting father and husband. Tragically, he would be dead from cancer within two years of this defeat. He played through his illness, and the bruising effects of chemotherapy, but there was to be no respite.

Jimmy was playing in a charity match when he received the news about Hunter's death. A man had paid £10,000 for the honour of playing Jimmy that night. At one point during the match Jimmy looked over at his PA and thought he seemed a bit strange, but he didn't learn the news about Hunter until the match was over. He felt sick to hear that his 27-year-old "little friend" had passed away.

As well as being a sensational player, Hunter sexed snooker up the way Tony Knowles had in the 1980s. In the 2001 Masters he trailed Fergal O'Brien 6-2 at the first interval and decided on a novel manner of reviving his flagging spirits: He adjourned to the boudoir of his hotel with his fiancé. It seemed to work because he came out that evening and knocked in four centuries en route to beating O'Brien 10-9. Steve Davis, giving an example of his great wit, coined an immortal phrase when he said, "The post-session interval turned into the post-interval session!"

Paul Hunter is sadly missed by everybody in the game, especially Jimmy, who was emotional at his funeral. Sometimes I wonder if Hunter didn't try as hard as he might have during that final with Jimmy, happy that his friend had come back from the brink to secure another (last?) title. He wouldn't have handed it to him on a platter but, like the rest of us, would quietly muse that it couldn't have happened to a nicer guy. Truly, it took one to know one.

But as ever with Jimmy, where there was good, bad followed. A rumour surfaced that Jimmy was snorting cocaine. The story garnered the kinds of headlines one imagined were a thing of the past for this man. Following this, during a trip to Ireland, his appendix became inflamed and he had to have it removed in County Roscommon. Not surprisingly, he became the darling of the nurses, who accepted it as just another event in the turbulent life of Jimmy White.

Jimmy failed to reach the quarter-finals of any tournament during the 2004/05 season, but still rose three places in the rankings to be in the top eight once again. This was mainly due to his sterling performances during the 2003/04 season and others' failings. His popularity was growing again with vociferous audiences urging their man on. Shortly before the World Championships began in 2004, Will Buckley wrote in the *Guardian* that the public would never forgive Hendry for beating Jimmy four times at the Crucible. 'It's not his fault,' Buckley wrote, 'but he would be more popular if he'd thrown one of those finals – not for money, but for other people's love.'

Jimmy, he said, was loved not only for his easy charm but also his 'instinctive dignity in the aftermath of so many defeats.' He was 'the last punk sportsman' and had managed to combine 'the attitude of Joe Strummer with the longevity of Keith Richards'. Whether he won at Sheffield or not, Buckley contended, Jimmy should be celebrated just for being there. And celebrate Jimmy's fans did, until he lost 10-8 to Barry Pinches in the first round.

Prior to that year's Masters there was much newspaper coverage of Jimmy's over-exuberant fans. The *Guardian* revealed that extra security guards were being recruited for the tournament. This was to prevent the recurrence of an incident the previous year in which a selection of Jimmy's supporters decided to break wind – perhaps appropriately for a Whirlwind – just at the moment when his opponents were down on their shots, thereby destroying their concentration. "The farters will not be tolerated," Jimmy announced reassuringly. Maybe not, but there was more than one way to skin a cat – or a Scot.

When Jimmy played Hendry at the 2003 Masters there had been many boos directed at Hendry before the match began. This was London, after all, not Sheffield, where the Scot was tolerated by Jimmy's fans, at least ostensibly. But Wembley always had a big fight atmosphere to it. Jimmy won the match 6-4 and went on to beat Ebdon in the quarter-final before going down to Ronnie O'Sullivan in the semis.

Jimmy started 2005 in fighting mood. "I'm now involved as soon as the gun goes off," he said. "In the past it took me two or three rounds to get the adrenalin rush." He said he'd sworn off cigarettes to help his cause, adding, "I've been smoking all my life so if I can stop that I can do anything."

He faced Hendry in the opening match of the Premier League that year. He appealed to his fans not to be too noisy, remembering the way they'd been at the 2003 Masters. He actually threatened to quit the game if there was a repeat of that. "Even darts players are getting angered with shouting," he said. Maybe on the throw, but asking darts supporters to be quiet would surely be like asking people at a football match to hush when the visiting team is taking a penalty in front of the home end.

The 2005 Masters was controversial, but for a different reason. Jimmy made the strange decision to change his name from White to Brown during the tournament. His motive for this was to highlight the role of HP brown sauce in subsidising the tournament. There were rumours he'd keep the name change right through the season, but thankfully this didn't come to pass. "It's an idea to put the fun back into snooker," he explained, and he donned a brown jacket to play his matches instead of the usual black one. If he won the tournament he promised to have the name Jimmy Brown engraved on the trophy.

This didn't happen, though Jimmy produced a near-miraculous recovery against Matthew Stevens to reach the quarter-finals of the event. He was 4-1 down at one point. He won a subsequent frame after needing two snookers. For Stevens it was more heartache in a frightful season. Jimmy knew he hadn't played well, but was happy to accept the victory.

The next round was like black comedy against Mark Williams. Jimmy went 3-0 up, but Williams complained that the cushions were springy so the mid-session interval was declared a frame early. After they resumed, Williams seized the initiative to level at 3-3. Jimmy eventually won a final frame which boasted a highest break of, wait for it, 14. "I was coming apart at the seams," he declared after the match, "but if you've got to win ugly, do it." (Why hadn't someone told him that in Sheffield in 1992?) Ronnie O'Sullivan overcame him 6-1 in the semi-final.

Jimmy beat Fergal O'Brien in the first round of the World Championships that year. In the next round he found himself up against Matthew Stevens once again. He'd beaten Stevens on the last few occasions they'd played, but the Welshman was in a mean mood and after sharing the first few frames with Jimmy ran into an overnight 12-4 lead which was insurmountable. Jimmy, as ever, looked on the bright side of an abysmal performance, saying he hoped he'd be in the top eight for the 2005/06 season. As for his fans, they were now fearing they may have seen the last of the Whirlwind on the big stage.

But Jimmy had often surprised us when he was written off like this. And he did so again, albeit fleetingly. In October 2005, he rolled back the years, hammering Ricky Walden 5-2 to move into the last 16 of the Grand Prix in Preston. This was in part thanks to what he laughingly referred to as a "humungous fluke" in the sixth frame. ("I don't get many of them, you know," he laughed afterwards.) Jimmy was now ranked 8th in the world, but 23rd on the provisional list. He needed to build on this for the rest of the season.

Shortly after the Grand Prix Jimmy suggested that he was thinking of joining Ronnie O'Sullivan on the American 8-ball pool circuit. O'Sullivan had declared that snooker was losing its appeal and needed to shift direction. Jimmy agreed that the game was being run "by muppets" and needed a shot in the arm. The talent was there ("Every night 10 or 11 kids turn up in their bow ties and waistcoats to play me, and they can all make centuries"), but there was something dull about the governing body's approach. This was perhaps the reason the sponsors for the game were drying up, and why as a result only five ranking tournaments were scheduled for the coming year. Jimmy and Ronnie shifted their attention to the International Pool Tour, the brainchild of billionaire Kevin Trudeau, whose own company, NaturalCures.com, was funding it. "He wants to make snooker like the Super Bowl," said Ronnie, "and I couldn't help but get excited."

Whether it was the diversion of pool or simply age, Jimmy's decline in form started soon afterwards, at the end of 2005. He trailed Ding Jun Hui 8-0 in the second round of the UK Championship and eventually went down 9-3. The following month he was beaten 6-3 by John Higgins in the Masters at Wembley. In February 2006 he was whitewashed 5-0 by Ryan Day in the Welsh Open. Next he was beaten by Andrew Higginson, the world No. 77, 5-3 in the third qualifying round of the Malta cup in Prestatyn in March, having failed to qualify for the final stages of the season's first two ranking events, the Northern Ireland Trophy and the Grand Prix. He let a 3-1 lead slip against Higginson, losing four frames on the spin to crash out of the event.

More significantly, Jimmy was humbled 10-5 by David Gray in the first round of the World Championships. He was now in danger of dropping out of the top 32. "The table was abysmal," he carped, "it was running off all over the shop." But maybe a more bitter truth was in his own game. "I never got going," he confessed.

Traditionally Jimmy had never moaned about such things. Was this an indication that his ability was now permanently on the wane? The evidence seemed to support this theory. In November 2006 he was beaten 9-4 by Finland's Robin Hull in the final qualifying round of the UK Championships in Prestatyn, causing him to fall further in the rankings. The 9am start wasn't to Jimmy's liking, but by now one felt he'd need a minor miracle to claw his way back into the top flight of the game.

His misery was compounded when Ronnie O'Sullivan beat him 7-0 the following month in the Premier League final at Wythenshawe Forum. Ronnie was unstoppable, knocking in breaks of 122, 93, 73 and 113 on his way to the victory,

It made him the first player since Davis to win the League on three straight occasions. He'd also whitewashed Hendry 6-0 in the League final the previous year and had beaten Mark Williams by the same margin in the 2004/05 season. It was Jimmy's first appearance in a final since winning the 2004 Player's Championship. He took some solace in getting that far, having beaten Graeme Dott in the semis, but knew he wasn't at the races in the final.

"I couldn't settle," was how Jimmy summed it up. "If you let Ronnie get on top of you it can be demoralising. That's what happened. I had no table time and that makes things impossible."

But surely there was more to it than this. Did he not need someone to dismantle his game (and even his mind) completely? The fans were still turning up in numbers, despite his dismal run of form. Everyone recognised his raw talent – but did he have the verve and the hunger, those intangibles which made him Jimmy White? That was the question we all wanted answering.

Hendry had never been averse to a bit of mentoring. Neither had Davis. Mark Williams recruited the services of Terry Griffiths to tell him where he was going wrong. Ronnie O'Sullivan himself took the septuagenarian Ray Reardon out of the wilderness to help him capture a second world title in 2004. These players have won 18 World Championships between them; Jimmy hadn't won any, but still resolutely refused to have his game or cue action analysed.

It got worse. The following month he was beaten again, this time 5-4 by Ireland's Mark Allen in the final qualifying round of the Welsh Open in Prestatyn. Later that month he showed flashes of his old brilliance in beating Nigel Bond 5-2 at the same venue to qualify for the final stages of the China Open, posting breaks of 93 and 70 in the process. But these flashes were becoming fewer and further between. In March 2007 he was denied a 26th appearance at Sheffield by Jamie Burnett in the penultimate qualifying round of the World Championships. He had only failed to appear at Sheffield once since 1981 (in 2001) and now stood 34th in the world rankings.

Jimmy had no excuses. "I didn't perform at all," he said. In what was by now almost a mandatory P.S., he added, "I'm devastated I couldn't produce the form I've been showing in practice." Burnett felt for his victim, saying, "It was hard for me because I'm a Jimmy White fan, but I had a job to do." As ever it seemed it hurt the victor as much to defeat Jimmy as it did the man himself to lose.

Unable to play at the finals in Sheffield, Jimmy actually went into the commentary box for the BBC studios that year, something I thought I'd never see. He sat beside the Scottish broadcaster Hazel Irvine, throwing pearls of wisdom at her like an after-dinner speaker. It was strange for me to hear a man who'd made so many elementary mistakes so often in his career acting like Mr Know-All.

Listening to all of this put me into a depression for some reason. I would have preferred to see Jimmy driving the car rather than dissecting the engine. That should have been left to the millions of us who couldn't make a 30 break.

In May 2007 Jimmy gave an interview to Robert Philip of the *Daily Telegraph*. Philip asked him how he felt being a commentator of the Sheffield action rather than a participator. "Working for the Beeb," Jimmy enthused, "has made me even more determined to qualify for next year's championship."

Philip asked him how he felt about Higgins considering they had an exhibition coming up. "I'm already planning my escape," Jimmy joked. "He's just finished a book and everyone in the snooker world is scared to open it. He's at war with everyone. He was a legend and now he's disowned." But the exhibition was still a sell-out. Both had so many loyal fans that there simply wasn't an arena big enough anywhere to house them. This despite Alex being 48 and Jimmy 45.

Philip's next question, perhaps inevitably, involved Ronnie O'Sullivan. Was he a tortured soul? "Yeah, but I've told him to behave himself. That's good coming from me, I know, but I probably know the right route even if I haven't always stuck to it."

Jimmy was still chipper about his chances of making a comeback to the top ranks of the game. Jack Nicklaus, after all, had won his sixth Masters at Jimmy's age. It was, he claimed, still possible for him to win a World title, but it was getting harder every year. "The players are younger and fitter. Ronnie can run a sub-six-minute mile. There are probably ten players who could win every year whereas there might have been two or three potential champions in the past."

But did he regret never yet winning the World title? Incredibly Jimmy answered with brutal honesty, the kind which burned holes through the hearts of so many of his fans who had watched him come so far and fall so near the finishing post: "My only regret is that I didn't prepare properly for the Crucible at times. I'm not being funny, but if I turned up to play someone like Dennis Taylor I thought I was so good I could beat him with my 'C' game. That's no way to become world champion."

Life, as they say, can only be understood backwards. But it has to be lived forwards.

THE PEOPLE'S CHAMPION

IN 2007 JIMMY went behind bars ... to play an exhibition match in Dublin's Mountjoy jail. He didn't take a fee as the money was going to Our Lady's Hospital for Sick Children in the suburb of Crumlin. "I'll play anyone," Jimmy announced. "As far as I know I'll be playing five prisoners and a prison officer."

Such was the demand to go up against him, the names had to be drawn from a hat. There were armed robbers, drug addicts, drug dealers, even a man accused of murder. "You name it," said a source, "and they're in here. He's their hero and they want to play him. This is the biggest thing to happen here in a long time. Jimmy is the People's Champion and people like him because he's so down to earth. The jail is buzzing with excitement."

Accompanied on the visit by his friend Alfie Burden, Jimmy played both snooker and pool against all comers. The games were played at the prison auditorium in front of 200 invited guests, with gang members segregated in case they caused trouble. Afterwards Jimmy went on a walkabout to meet more prisoners and prison officers as well as signing a few cues and, as he put it, "bits and bobs".

He told reporters he was waiting for the finishing touches to be put to a home he had bought in Kilcock, County Kildare, called Love Me Tender. "It's got four bedrooms and of course a snooker room," he said, "so I can practise for tournaments. I love Ireland. I've been coming here doing exhibition matches for the last 25 years, so I just decided to get up in the place."

More time in Ireland meant more time with Hurricane Higgins, of course. Wherever the pair of them went, controversy soon followed. During an exhibition match at the Spennymoore Snooker Centre, the referee Terry Riley adjudged Higgins to have fouled the blue with his shirt. Higgins reacted by hitting Riley in the stomach. The referee then grabbed Higgins by the neck and pushed him backwards along the table. Suddenly it was beginning to look like a wrestling bout rather than a game of snooker. All Jimmy could do was throw his head back and laugh.

The match continued for five more minutes (without Riley), at which point the promoter, Gary Astley, stopped it. He addressed the audience, saying, "Tonight was a unique event. I spent the last three months promoting it and this was not in the script. I don't care what anybody says, Alex is one of the nicest people I have met in my life."

He might have added, 'When he's not punching people.'

Higgins claimed that Riley overreacted. Riley said, "It was a punch and officials are not there to be punched." He had a point.

But it wasn't always fist-fights and piss-ups. In March 2008 Jimmy paired up with Higgins again, this time for an exhibition match in County Clare, Ireland, to raise funds for the Niall Mellon Township Trust. This is a charity which helps provide homes to poor communities in the townships of South Africa. It provides 20 per cent of the low cost homes in Cape Town and 15 per cent of houses in the Gauteng region. Tickets were £25 and VIP ones £50. The latter entitled holders to a champagne reception where they would meet and greet the players before the match. There was also an auction, the prize being an opportunity to play a frame against Jimmy or Alex.

The event was well attended and a roaring success, but within days Jimmy's warm glow had been shattered by another unfortunate event when his father died in November, aged 88. Had it finally broken that big heart of his to see another May slide by without his beloved son hoisting the Crucible trophy high in his arms?

Soon afterwards Jimmy was beaten 10-3 by Mark King in the last qualifying round for Sheffield, arguably his last realistic chance to appear in the Crucible. "I'm in shreds," was all Jimmy could say after the match.

He was conspicuous in the 2008 World finals by his absence. Or was he really absent? Jimmy had spawned a generation of players who had now taken over from him, so in truth he'll never be totally gone.

I saw him in Jamie Cope, who lost so gallantly to Peter Ebdon in the first round, and in Mark Allen, who also went out at that stage in a final-frame shoot-out with Hendry after blowing a big lead.

There always seem to be doggedly determined old stagers and exciting newcomers who just fail to convert winning opportunities. Maybe it will always be thus. People like Ebdon and Hendry always looked hungry when they needed snookers in a frame, as did Davis, whereas Jimmy, Ronnie and all the other 'flair' players dropped the head at these times. They didn't like hunting lost causes so much.

Before the tournament began Graeme Dott had revealed he was considering not playing as he was suffering from depression brought on by 15 successive defeats during the season and some health problems in his family. Stephen Lee was also feeling the pressure, losing out to Joe Swail, who surprisingly trounced him 10-4 in the first round. "I'm fed up unpacking my case and then packing it again the next day," Lee moaned. Jimmy would have known the feeling.

Steve Davis went out in the first round too, despite coming back from 8-3 down against Stuart Bingham to level at 8-8. He also looked likely to go 9-8 up before a poor positional shot from the final blue to pink, and a subsequent missed black, let Bingham in to snatch victory. As I watched Davis clawing his way back I thought of Jimmy. How many times had he made gallant fightbacks in the past, only to be foiled at the last fence. Surely Davis wasn't turning into Jimmy? Whether he was or not, it seemed to be a pattern with him in recent Sheffield encounters to let his opponents get away from him and then play great snooker to (almost) catch up.

Ronnie O'Sullivan won the 2008 tournament, defeating Ali Carter 18-8 in the final, to claim his third World title. A few days afterwards there was a story in the paper about Paul Gascoigne being on a path to self-destruction after a failed suicide bid. "That could have been me," Ronnie declared, adding, "Eight years ago, when I was low, I had the wrong characters around me. I put the brakes on and managed to sort myself out. I've become me again. You get a new circle of friends."

Jimmy had always seemed to be surrounded by dodgy people in his prime, deadbeats attaching themselves to his 24/7 party lifestyle and then leaving him to pick up the pieces afterwards. It was the reason Maureen said she was never worried about another woman with her husband, only another man.

Later that year a DVD called *There's Only One Jimmy White* came out. It was made by a company called Gangster Productions, which alerted you to the fact that it was going to be a somewhat freewheeling affair, as indeed it proved to be. It contained testimonials to Jimmy from anybody who was anybody, and showed him at work and play as he made one last bid to keep in the game. Ronnie O'Sullivan was one of the people interviewed. Asked to compare himself to Jimmy, Ronnie joked, "Well, they'll never give me an MBE!" He said he was a friend of Jimmy and loved playing him, but at Wembley the crowd was so partisan he was reminded of Monica Seles being stabbed by a Steffi Graf fan some years before. Jimmy had that kind of adulation in London, Ronnie wryly commented.

There was also some wild footage of Jimmy in a pub with his promoter Kevin Kelly. Kevin had a little too much to drink and at one point looked like he was going to wreck the bar. Jimmy playfully started to 'strangle' him with his tie to quieten him down. There was lots of 'language' from both of them, something I'd never heard Jimmy use this freely. Neither had I ever heard him use the threat of violence, even in jest. It was funny, but there was also something of a dark undertone in the episode. I had never been privy to this side of Jimmy and I wondered if it was something new that had developed within him after the years of being the Nearly Man, or whether this was the side of him that he kept deeply hidden but had perhaps prevented him reaching the pinnacle of the game.

Elsewhere Steve Davis compared Jimmy's 'cavalier' style of play to his own 'anal' one. People like Ken Doherty, Tony Drago, Willie Thorne and a host of others weighed in with superlatives about the man who had done everything in the game except bag 'the big one'. It was probably too late now, they agreed, but who wouldn't like to have six World finals (and eight semi-finals) on their CV? Jimmy himself, asked how he'd liked to be remembered, said wistfully "As world champion". The old devil still wasn't giving up, although it was clear to everyone else that the People's Champion would never in fact become world champion.

Towards the end of the video we see Jimmy at home with his adoring children. Lauren, his eldest daughter, praised his generosity. Tommy Tiger, his youngest child, said he was grumpy in the morning. Maureen, his ex-wife of four years, said she was still good friends with him and they met often for dinner but there was no chance of them getting back together. Jimmy agreed, but both seemed jolly about the fact. The 20-year relationship had run its course and neither was bitter about it ending. Both themselves and their children looked happier than many 'stable' households.

The DVD showed Jimmy playing in a few ranking matches as well, but it all seemed too little too late. He was cutting down on the wild living, but there was no doubt that time was running out for the Tooting legend. He wouldn't give up unless they dragged him away from the table. He loved the game, the buzz, the crowds, even 'Auntie Agatha' disturbing his concentration by unwrapping a sweet in the front row. It had been a brilliant ride but you felt that this was his swansong.

In an interview with Richard Bath in *The Scotsman* later in 2008 Jimmy made the point, "You can come through anything if you keep your sense of humour. I've had fun setting fire to several million quid." Asked about the prospect of retirement he philosophised, "Every sportsman has to come to the end of his career, but I feel I still have the game, so I can't put down my cue, not yet. I love to go and do exhibitions, I love travelling and I love playing once I get there. I feel I'm capable of playing to a good standard. The belief is still there."

Did he have any regrets? "Of course I wish I'd done certain things differently, but you can't go back. I've had a fantastic life, I've met fantastic people and I like to think I'll be remembered."

Asked about how his career panned out in general he reflected, "People say I'm the best player never to have won the World Championship, but I've won 10 ranking tournaments and 27 invitational ones. I wasn't exactly an early-to-bed person so I've done really well. As a kid my ambition was to be a snooker player so I'm living the dream. I still love the click of the balls and the noise around the table. As long as people want to come and see me play then I'll carry on."

He needn't worry, methinks. His fans would queue up to see him reading the phone book.

A CHARMED LIFE

THE LAST TIME I met Jimmy was a few years ago when he was in Drogheda to play an exhibition. He looked massive in bulk, in contrast to the skinny urchin of 1982. I remembered Steve Davis being asked once why he thought Jimmy's form declined over the years. He replied, "Jimmy is very big now." He meant in his frame. It was probably a roundabout way of saying Jimmy didn't exercise. It was well known Davis spent a lot of time in the gym keeping his physique fit. In this he pre-dated the new crop of players who set a lot of store by physical fitness (Ronnie O'Sullivan has been known to run up to ten miles on the day of a match.)

I asked Jimmy how he felt. Since I'd last met him he'd lost five World finals. "I'm buzzing," he chortled, as ever. You got the feeling that if Jimmy was sitting at the bottom of a ton of coal being dropped into a quarry and you asked him how he felt he'd say, "I'm buzzing." It was that unquenchable spirit Thorburn alluded to when he said, "Win or lose, Jimmy is unfazed." But for some reason it annoyed me. It smacked of denial. I remembered Mike Hallett saying once that he only played well when he was angry with himself. Maybe Jimmy could have done with a bit of that anger.

I made some flippant comment about his great achievements since we last met. "I've had my moments," he smiled, so I chanced asking him if he had any regrets. "Not really. You have to play it like you see it. I've had a giggle. It's easy to look back and beat yourself up for things, but I don't do that."

What about the drink? "What about it!" he replied.

I asked him if he'd have taken less if it meant he'd won the World title. "Of course I'd have taken bloody less! But it's easy to say that now. It's cost me a few matches – and a few nicker. But I wouldn't change anything. I've had a charmed life."

It was the same old Jimmy. You had to admire him for his positive thinking even if it was blinkered. I couldn't think of anything else to say except to wish him well in the exhibition. He said to come over to him afterwards and we'd have a little chat if he had time.

As ever, the audience, who were crackling with anticipation at the opportunity of watching Jimmy in action, were ecstatic when he started to play, applauding anything vaguely smacking of excitement. He was potting them from all angles and putting a lot of action on the cue ball. At one point of the night the barman dropped a huge tray of drinks and caused an almighty clatter behind Jimmy. He stopped playing and looked around him. "I didn't know Alex Higgins was here," he said and the audience erupted. The magic was still there.

After the match was over I told him I was writing a book about him. I asked him if he'd like to collaborate. He said, "Maybe". He took a piece of paper out of his pocket and wrote a mobile telephone number on it. "Don't show that to nobody else," he said, "but ring me on it."

It ended with the digits 147, such a Jimmy touch.

I left the venue that night feeling ten feet tall, but when I rang the number a few days later it just rang out. Once again the Artful Dodger had eluded me.

THERE'S ONLY ONE

JIMMY WHITE

BUT WAS THAT it? Jimmy made a very promising start to the 2008/09 season, winning all of his six qualifying matches at Pontin's. He also qualified for the Shanghai Masters by beating Ken Doherty (also out of the top 16 for the first time since he went professional) by 5 frames to 1.

This seemed a new, changed Jimmy. In recent years he had become a much mellower specimen than in his wilder days. No doubt he realised world glory was beyond him, but he was still in there 'punching', as he put it. In the dogfights of the Prestatyn qualifiers where he engaged with hungry young lions anxious to take the Whirlwind's scalp he took whatever was thrown at him. Having gambled away his wealth, if not his talent, he was still up for the scrap.

In that meeting in Drogheda Jimmy opened up to me about the lifestyle he'd lived. "When I was drinking I'd only go to bed when the laughing stopped, but the problem was, I always had such a good time that the laughing went on all night. I'd find places that gangsters couldn't get to open. I had that knack of getting landlords and nightclub owners to open or stay open. It was carnage, but I had a good time."

Jimmy also spoke about his addiction to gambling: "I was compulsive. One day it would be dogs, then horses, then cards, then casinos. I was a binge gambler and only stopped when I went skint, which I did a few times."

He admitted that when he lost the 1994 final to Hendry by the odd frame at the Crucible he blew the whole second place prize money (£128,000) at the bookies. Afterwards he went to the TV hypnotist Paul McKenna, who "helped cure me of drugs, drink, gambling, smoking and women." That's one heck of a shopping list.

Life is different for Jimmy now than it used to be. He doesn't get thrown out of hotel rooms any more, or arrested at riots. He drinks in moderation and doesn't go AWOL at boring gigs. The effervescent urchin has become a venerable gent, the ferocious potter of yesteryear a fearful tactician. Of course it happens to all players, but with Jimmy somehow it's harder to take in. For a time he looked like he was going to live fast, die young and make a good-looking corpse like his lookalike and namesake Jimmy Dean. But this Jimmy never does what you expect.

Family man? Nah. MBE? Hardly. World snooker champion? Okay, I'll get back to you on that one.

When I sat down to think about writing this book, the first thing I realised were the conclusions I'd draw from my 30 years following this fascinating man's career. I knew that the things that made him great were also the things that made him fail. Think Alex Higgins. Think George Best, Elvis Presley, Sid Vicious, Marilyn Monroe and anyone else that was heady with the slipstream of sudden success and let it derail their first intentions. But unlike those luminaries Jimmy's still on the planet, three wheels on his wagon, and still in love with the game that defined him and that he helped define. He can say, like the American poet Charles Bukowski wrote, 'What the hell, I had it for a while. That beats the other.'

Few people really understand the pressures of snooker, or indeed any game played at the top level. In his book *Pocket Money*, Gordon Burn writes of a young player called Mark Thompson who committed suicide some years ago at the age of 19 because things weren't happening for him fast enough. We all know what happened to Alex Higgins. Ronnie O'Sullivan has been in the Priory for depression and related problems.

But not Jimmy.

Jimmy wrote in his autobiography: 'If you hit the white ball straight and true, the shot you're going for will work. If you hit it wrong or give just the tiniest bit too much side, bend, spin, or dip, from the moment it leaves the tip of your cue it's a round rolling bomb.'

He went on to add, significantly, that the said bomb 'doesn't explode near the target you missed. It explodes inside you.' In other words you die a bit after a costly error and it infuses everything you do afterwards in a match – or don't do. This is particularly applicable to Jimmy, who personifies a simultaneous kind of laconicism mixed with high nervous energy at the table. Clive James once described him as having 'the nervous system of a fighter pilot on amphetamines'.

On the face of it Jimmy hasn't done badly. He's still healthy, he's also still one of the most popular sportsmen in Britain, as exemplified by being installed as the bookies' favourite when the list of contestants for the 2009 edition of ITV's hit reality TV show *I'm A Celebrity ... Get Me Out Of Here!* were announced in November of that year. And he's survived a cancer scare. The marriage may have gone west, and he's overweight, but he's still playing, even if that's primarily in exhibitions now. Many other players – Joe Johnson, Martin Clark, Chris Small, to name but a few, have had their careers cut short due to medical concerns, while Paul Hunter is no longer with us, and neither are Bill Werbeniuk or Cliff Wilson. Dean Reynolds had to give up the game due to a drink problem. Silvino Francisco ended his career serving a prison term for possession of cannabis after financial debts pushed him to this desperate stratagem.

There's another way of looking at Jimmy's infamous losing record in Crucible finals. Most of the players who remain in the top 8 for any length of time (if not the top 16) usually win the World title at least once. Jimmy didn't, but would he have preferred to be a Joe Johnson, who then paid the price a hundredfold by developing heart problems as a result?

Having met Jimmy and got to know him just a wee bit, I don't think he would. Terry Griffiths says he was snubbed at his local club in Llanelli after he went back there as world champion. This would hardly have happened to Jimmy in London, but you never know. "Fame doesn't change you as much as it does the people around you," Jimmy told me. And he should know. He's been burned too many times by the sting of publicity.

Would we still feel the same about Jimmy if he'd nicked that last frame off Stephen Hendry in 1994? Would he be heading into ITV's jungle as their headline act amongst a cast of wannabees and has-beens? For you can be sure that Jimmy is still the star attraction wherever he goes.

It's sad that most people remember him more for things he did wrong (the two disasters against Hendry in Sheffield in 1992 and 1994, the rash green against Davis in the 1982 final and the rest shot against Higgins two years before) than his incredible victories. The tag of bridesmaid at the Sheffield wedding is one that affixes itself to him like a piece of chewing gum on his shoe.

But you can be certain that this lovable, infuriating, wonderful, idiosyncratic, dashing gem of a player will command people's hearts for ever and a day. Isn't that worth a World title in anyone's currency?

* * *

Nearing 50, Jimmy is now on the verge of retirement. Theoretically he could stay on the circuit for another year or so, like his old enemy Steve Davis, who's still playing quite well, despite an ignominious first round defeat in the World Championships by Neil Robertson in 2009. "When my world ranking is higher than my age," Davis kids, "I'll retire." (He's 51.) Jimmy's ranking has been higher than his age for a number of years now, but he's still hanging in there.

Snooker is a very different game today than it was when Jimmy came into the pro ranks in 1980. At that time only a few players dominated the top flight. Today, as in golf, any one of a dozen players is capable of winning a major. When you consider the number of World titles won by Joe Davis, his brother Fred, John Pullman, John Spencer, Ray Reardon, Steve Davis and Stephen Hendry from the beginning of the century to the end, you're talking of an average of perhaps six titles to a given player. That would be unthinkable today. Only Ronnie O'Sullivan and John Higgins among the current crop has three world titles to their name. Mark Williams comes next with two. Everyone else only has one ... except, of course, Jimmy.

The standard of play has also improved vastly as the game has developed and become, dare we say it, more professional. "Every player is 20 points better than the players of the last generation," a certain scallywag from Tooting believes. I'd suggest he could add at least another ten on toCthat.

Today's players also have the benefits of being able to learn from television, an avenue that wasn't open to Jimmy's generation. They had to learn by watching players in the flesh. Or in Jimmy's case, by instinct. Sometimes that instinct let him down, which is perhaps the story of this book, and his life. But when it didn't he was riveting. And, as I've been at pains to point out, even when he did fall short he was still, as they put it in his manor, a different gravy.

You pays your money and you takes your choice, as the Americans say. Would we prefer Davis and Hendry, the Steady Eddies with their 13 World titles between them, or the brilliant but unreliable Jimmy who brought us to the brink so many times before imploding? Maybe it depends on whether you see snooker as theatre or not. I think it should be. Why else would the World Championships of the sport be held at a venue which is, for the remaining 50 weeks of the year, a theatre? For me that also means that the trophies in one's cabinet should come second to one's ability to entertain and captivate.

Now in the autumn (winter?) of his career, I hope Jimmy continues to go for the tasty pot above the safety shot. He has nothing to lose now and it would be a pity if he were to fold his tent in a manner unbecoming of the Whirlwind. I don't think it's likely. He was always in the game because of his love of playing snooker, not simply for any of its ancillary benefits.

"Even if there wasn't any money in this game," he told me, "I'd still be down in the snooker hall with my mates. Snooker is my life." It's also his job, and therein lies the problem, because jobs need to be finished. In the words of snooker commentator Jack Karnehm, Jimmy is "a beautiful boxer without a knockout punch".

In the qualifiers for the Welsh Open in 2009 Jimmy beat Rod Lawler 5-4 and David Grace by the same margin before demolishing Ken Doherty 5-0. The Lawler match was particularly memorable as he came back from 4-0 down to win. When the tournament reached the televised stages, however, he crumbled against Ali Carter, its eventual winner, getting dumped out 5-1 in a lacklustre match. "Carter has a lot of respect for Jimmy," remarked Eurosport's commentator David Hendon, "but the arena is no place for sympathy."

Jimmy got a magical standing ovation when he walked in to play that match – let's not forget it had been a long time since he'd appeared on television – but that was really as good as it got. He never really looked like winning. Being out of the pressure cooker environment of the television latter stages of a tournament for as long as he was can't have helped, but he'd been doing exhibitions with Higgins and O'Sullivan to keep his hand in. In fact shortly before the Carter match both himself and Ronnie knocked in a 147 each in one such exhibition.

While there is the allure of Sheffield to keep him going, Jimmy will never give in. On 27 February 2009 he lost to Andy Hicks in the qualifiers for the World Championships by 10 frames to 8. Ironically, 10-8 had also been his losing scoreline against Davis at Sheffield in 1981, the first season of his professional career. Somehow the Hicks score seemed to be a fitting valedictory. Things ended as they began. The wheel had come full circle. What goes around comes around.

But whether your take on Jimmy White's colourful life is that he fulfilled and thrilled or burned and spurned his talent there's no doubt that along the way he won the hearts and admiration of pretty much everyone he came into contact with. Even the greatest snooker player in the world was a hardened Jimmy White fan. Some years ago during a recording at the BBC of a *This Is Your Life* special for Stephen Hendry, Jimmy handed the Scotsman a £1 note with written on it the words 'From Jimmy White to the new Jimmy White'. Hendry sent it back with another inscription: 'There's only one Jimmy White.'

How right he was.